Y0-BRJ-198

Burgess

CAMPING SERIES

Consulting Editors
BARBARA ELLEN JOY and MARJORIE CAMP

THE CAMP COUNSELOR'S BOOK

God give me sympathy and sense
And help me keep my courage high;
God give me calm and confidence
And please, a twinkle in my eye.

Mary S. Edgar

The

CAMP COUNSELOR'S

Book

edited by

MARY L. NORTHWAY

and

BARRY G. LOWES

Burgess Publishing Company

426 South 6th Street • Minneapolis 15, Minnesota

The quatrain by Mary S. Edgar used as the epigraph of this book is quoted from *Under Open Skies* by permission of the publishers, Clarke, Irwin & Company Limited.

Contents

Introduction

THIS is a book for camp counselors. The writers have all been counselors themselves and most of them are now camp directors, so they not only know what your job will be like, but they remember how it feels to be a camp counselor. All the writers are Canadian, but what they say is certainly not limited to Canadian camping. It should blow like a fresh, clear breeze from Canada to all places in the world wherever organized camping exists.

As Canadians we have followed usage based on the Oxford Dictionary—except for the one word *counselor*. Camp leadership developed in the United States, and the term *camp counselor* originated there. This origin is acknowledged by our use of the American spelling.

Camps of course differ greatly, in location, length of period, age, sex of the campers, background, fees, policies, and program. Also, the particular activity you will assist with may vary from teaching swimming to helping in the office. However, regardless of what kind of camp you go to or what your special job is, your key function as a counselor is to take charge of a small cabin group of children, who will be the focus of your responsibility, your interest, and, we hope, your delight. This book is designed to help you understand and work with your own special group, in their day-to-day living and as they participate in the larger camp program. To them you are the most important adult in the camp. You are a bit of a father, mother, teacher, friend, and mentor. You are something of all of these, yet fully none of them; you are their *counselor*—the person whose chief concern is the well-being and genuine personality growth of your own campers. The greatest need for growing children is adults who care; who support, encourage and comfort them and have infinite faith in their possibilities. As a counselor your purpose is to try to answer this need.

This book does not presume to tell you exactly what to do in your camp, where the practices may be different from those we describe, though equally good. Its purposes, rather, are to help you think about those things that concern counselors and their groups in all camps, and to give you a jumping-off place for discussion of how these may best be handled in your camp. Also, this book may well be used in camp training courses at which counselors from many different camps meet to learn what desirable camp practices are. Of course, it may be that even camp directors will glean an idea or two from it!

To produce a book requires the efforts of many people, in addition to the writers whose names appear at the top of the chapters. Professor Dorothy Millichamp of the Institute of Child Study, University of Toronto, gave a great deal of help with the chapter *Understanding Your Campers,* and also read the entire manuscript. Miss Marie Milton edited the rough drafts and organized the Institute secretaries, Mrs. Jill Oman and Mrs. Erma Ross, on the typing of the final manuscript. Miss Jean Quinn worked on many aspects of the whole process, and Miss Catherine Beith took charge of my household, freeing me to work on the final phases of the manuscript. Mrs. Dorothy Douglas, editor of *Canadian Camping*, compiled and checked the bibliography.

We hope you will find this book valuable and that it will

help you to become an excellent counselor; we hope too that at camp you will grow towards maturity—and that you will have fun. To let Barry Lowes have the last word:

"A counselor never knows how far his influence will spread. The greatest single factor in determining the happiness and success of any summer is you, the counselor. It is a tremendous responsibility that you take on. If it seems too great, do not become a camp counselor. But if you have the courage, the vision, the ability to learn, then come on in, the water's fine. You won't be left to sink or swim. There are many hands to help you. Beware, though, for camp is an infectious disease, and, once you catch it, it will be in your blood for life!"

Good camping to you!

M.L.N.

University of Toronto
January, 1963.

PART I

You and Your Campers

Chapter One

BECOMING A CAMP COUNSELOR

Mary L. Northway

IF YOU are considering becoming a camp counselor, you should realize that working with campers is becoming a profession; and, like any other profession, it presents certain opportunities and has certain requirements. Your decision will be more clearly made if you are aware of what the main opportunities and requirements are and how they will affect you; so we will discuss some aspects of a counselor's job which you should consider, ways in which you should seek a camp position, what is involved in accepting an appointment on a camp staff, and, finally, some values counseling has for you.

THINGS TO CONSIDER IN BECOMING A CAMP COUNSELOR

When you ask, "Shall I go to camp and, if so, what camp shall I go to?" you should be aware that in becoming a counselor you are accepting a *job*. The job provides a very pleasant outdoor summer with congenial companions and is a real change from indoor winter work. But a summer hotel would provide many of these things without the special duties counseling involves. The job usually provides remuneration, part of which may or may not be an actual salary cheque; but in many camps this cheque is not as great as one could obtain working in the city. However, you should realize that in addition to your salary you will receive board, lodging, and the use of good equipment and facilities for which you would have to pay a high sum in other circumstances, plus a good deal of in-service training. If you are willing to do a purposeful job in pleasant surroundings for a fairly low salary, at least when you start, then you should consider camp counseling. If you stay with camping and rise in position, your salary will become correspondingly greater.

There are two things which are essential if you are going to choose counseling: you should like children and you should like camping. If children bother you and you are impatient with their simplicities, or if you consider that living in the outdoors is unpleasant, better choose something else. Also, if you are to be a real counselor and not just a junior assistant, good camps will require that you are at least eighteen, have had some previous experience with children and in outdoor living, and have developed some teaching skills by which you can contribute to the activities of the camp community.

Camp counselors are either the home-grown variety, or imported. The former have grown up in the camp to which they return as leaders; the latter may or may not have camped, but are attracted to counseling, possibly because of their interest in such social professions as teaching, medicine, or psychology, or because of their skills in some activities of the camp—riding, swimming, archery, music.

If you are the home-grown variety, some time in advance your director and you will plan your program for becoming a leader. He may not want you to jump from camper to counselor directly. Possibly he will advise you to spend a year as a counselor-in-training. You might well discuss with him the wisdom of spending a summer at a different camp, or in another occupation, or taking summer courses that will broaden your experience. If you have been a camper for many years, a gap of a summer is often a good thing; you

4

return more mature, with a wider perspective and with an extra year between you and those who used to be your camper buddies. A camper should discuss his plans with his director if he aims to be a camp counselor.

If you have not grown up in a camp, you will probably inquire about camps from your friends, from camp directors and counselors whom you know, from organizations to which you belong which include camping in their activities, or from your teachers at school or at university. If you are taking a particular course, your teachers may be able to suggest camps whose activities and interests are particularly valuable to your career. Then too, you can consult the camping association of your province or state. It may have a counselors' bureau to which you can send your application, or a directory of the camps giving the main information about each so that you can apply directly.

Here are some questions you should ask yourself when selecting a camp:

> Is it a short-term or a long-term camp? Do I want to be away for two weeks, or for eight?
>
> Where is it located?
>
> What is its general policy? Has it a formal, regimented basis, is it a free-choice, loosely organized camp, or does it fall somewhere between? This is a matter of basic importance, for while you may be happy at one type of camp, the other may make you miserable.
>
> Are there any religious or racial limitations?
>
> Does it specialize in any particular activities—riding, canoe trips, dramatics, etc.—for which I have special ability?
>
> Do I know anyone who is going or has gone there?
>
> What is the attitude of former counselors to the camp?
>
> What is the salary range? Will it be a good experience for me in terms of my career? Some camps increase

salaries quite rapidly; what are the chances of promotion?

How to Go About Obtaining a Camp Position

When you have selected a few camps in which you are interested, you should write an application to the camp director as early as possible. Directors receive hundreds of applications each year. Among these there are some so illegible they cannot be deciphered, some with no date, no return address, no information about the writer, and occasionally no signature. All these are thrown into the wastepaper basket.

Your letter should be brief, giving name, street address and city, phone number, date, request for an application form, and the time you are available for an interview. Enclose a *brief* outline of your qualifications under the following headings: age, general background, present school grade, camp experience, special qualifications, and experience with children. This outline should give specific information in a straightforward, concise way.

If the director feels there is any possibility of using you at his camp he will arrange an interview, at which time he will find out all he can about you. At this interview you should get as many particulars as possible about the camp and also try to understand the director's general policies and point of view.

This may be the first time you have been interviewed for a job. Many books have been written on how to behave when applying for a job. The bare essentials are: be there on time; be frank, direct, and natural. Remember, an interview is a two-way affair—the director is learning as much as he can about you, but it is also your opportunity to find out all you can about the camp and what your job will entail. It's up to you to answer the director's questions honestly and without bluff, but also to ask him what you want to know about the camp. You should take a list of questions with you, so you won't forget in the limited time allowed for the interview.

Some of the things you will want to ask at this interview are:

> The opening and closing dates for your job; these may not be the same as the camp period. There may be a pre- or a post-camp staff session, or both.
>
> Salary and what this includes—transportation, laundry, use of equipment; are riding and water-skiing extras?
>
> Your duties as a group counselor and in activities; other duties—for example, water patrol, morning talks, night duty; rest hour.
>
> Living quarters—do you share a cabin with the campers? What are staff quarters like?
>
> Regulations regarding time off, smoking in camp and on days off, drinking (never in camp, but what about on time off?), hitch-hiking, taking your own car.
>
> What should you take by way of personal possessions —will your trumpet be welcome and your gun taboo?

It is through these specific questions that you will try to get an idea of what the camp stands for, what the director's purposes are, what he will expect of you, and how you feel about it all. He also will be sizing you up and appraising how well he thinks you will fit into his camp. If you don't like the regulations or the policies and feel you cannot accept them, this is the time to withdraw; *you* have to choose. If the regulations at this camp say *no* smoking and you like to smoke, you either decide to give up smoking for the summer, or you apply to a camp which is more liberal in its policy.

At this interview you might well ask what age group you will likely be working with, and state with what age children you have had most experience and feel most confident.

If the interview is satisfactory to the director and to you, he may indicate some pre-camp preparation he wishes you to make. He may suggest reading, or recommend a counselor's training course, or he may notify you of some special events in the city, such as swimming demonstrations, children's plays or art exhibits, nature rambles, or perhaps meetings of the camping association. These are valuable and should be attended if possible.

What Is Involved in Accepting an Appointment on a Camp Staff

The counselor's contract with the camp, whether made verbally or in writing, is expected to be kept in letter and in spirit. In addition to this a loyalty to the camp, its aims and policies, will be expected. Once you belong to the staff of a camp, unfavourable criticism about it should be reduced to a minimum. If you feel there is injustice to you, or neglect or malpractices in any aspect of the program, you should discuss these with the director and clarify the issues. Griping to other staff members has no place in camp. Nor should you disparage the camp to the general public. If you dislike some things about a camp so much that you cannot tolerate them, you should resign.

A counselor does not belong to one camp only. As soon as you accept a position on a staff, you become a part of the whole camping movement. Your attitude to camping will affect the movement and you can do much to interpret the aims of camping to the public. If you attend meetings of your local camping association before you go to camp, you will of course learn a good deal from the experts through their addresses and discussions. You will also see a great many displays of camp materials and books.

Equally important is the fact that you will meet people from many, many kinds of camp, not only from the type to which you are going, private camps, co-educational camps, nursery camps; organization camps, campfire girls, CGIT., Scouts, Y's; camps for welfare purposes, special camps for the crippled, blind or deaf, may all be represented. Catch a vision of the breadth of camping, and take it along with you to your own camp. Avoid insularity. Follow this up if possible during the summer by taking opportunities to visit other camps in your vicinity and to learn how they function. Camps at present, fortunately, differ greatly from each other; they have not fallen into a standardized pattern.

Some of the differences between other camps and your own may strike you as peculiar, and because of your emotional attachment to your own camp, you may be apt to think the practices at other camps less desirable. Some, of course, *will* be less desirable; some may be more. Keep these thoughts to yourself. Discuss some of the differences at counselors' meetings. Remember camps are partners, not rivals, and co-operative understanding of one another's practices is necessary if good camping standards are to evolve.

While you are employed by a camp, *you represent it*. This is true whether you are on duty or not. Camps try very hard to establish good public relations, especially in the neighbourhood and in nearby towns. Short-short shorts and unrequested entertaining with loudest camp songs in the village are rarely appreciated; speeding in a car or boat and running up bills at local stores are of course strictly taboo.

Respect for the property of neighbours and cottagers is essential. Permission to use it may be given to your director, and you must see that the lender's kindliness is respected. Unfortunately, a camp's reputation is often based on the thoughtlessness of an occasional counselor. A farmer whose wheat is trodden down, or a cottager who finds a fire left glowing on his beach or his birch trees stripped, will find little good to say about camping, and may refuse in future to let campers use his land. Take care of neighbours' property as you would your own, and remember that the cottagers are on their summer holidays and appreciate your courtesy and consideration of their enjoyment.

Your attitude to the local people is important. They may be different from your city acquaintances, but they are not stupid and they are not insensitive. You can learn a great deal from them and their ways of life. But a counselor who plays the role of a city slicker will not. Listening to old-timers' tales, to farmers' opinions on current affairs, to accounts of the interests and enterprises of the townsfolk, will enlarge your understanding immensely. Counselors who act superciliously, arrogantly or rudely to local folk are only displaying their own lack of security. You are probably interested in the community and are prepared to act at all times as a representative of your camp, but a person who does not have these attitudes should seek other employment.

VALUES OF BEING A CAMP COUNSELLOR

The immediate values of being a counselor for a summer are months of enjoyment in happy surroundings, health and zest, and usually a cheque in the pocket with which to start the autumn in the city.

Also you will have memories of sparkling blue days and white sails in the sunshine, of dramatic shows which you helped to produce, of counselors' evening parties, of toast and jam and much conversation, of jokes and fun, of amusing episodes with the campers, of long trips to unknown lakes, of interesting people and real friends. Through these you will have grown, learned new things, and taken real responsibility; you will have developed ideas and carried them out. You will have helped Johnny to solve his problems and Jane to realize her ideas, you will have developed a deeper understanding of children and a wider ability for approaching life maturely and co-operatively.

One important value will be that you will have met many

interesting adults from different occupations and professions, some of them distinguished in their own field. From them you may have become clearer about what you want as a vocation, what it entails and how to go about entering it. Many young people have chosen careers from discussions around a camp-fire. Your actual experience in camping will be a tremendous help in going through for a profession that involves people. In short, at the end of the summer you will find not only that you have been of value to your camp, but that your camp has been equally of value to you.

Chapter Two

UNDERSTANDING YOUR CAMPERS

Mary L Northway

GROWING TOWARDS MATURITY

SOME of your campers will be easier for you to understand than others. Some remind you of what you think you were like at their age; others reflect your ideas of what a child should be; still others have a special appeal because they are interested in the same activities as you are, or perhaps because they appreciate your talents or your jokes. And of course you are rarely baffled by children with whom your plans and techniques work; your success shows that for them your methods are right.

Some other campers you find more difficult to understand. Your plans do not work smoothly with them. Some are different from yourself or what you expect a child to be. These campers may have come from a different background or had a different upbringing, and the way they talk, think, and behave or misbehave is strange to you. Some you may feel are uninteresting and dull because they are not intrigued with things that interest you; and some may like to sit, while you believe that everyone should be energetic and make the most out of every shining moment. Others frighten you because they appear to know the ropes better than you do; this is particularly true if the boy is a very old camper and you are a very new counselor. Or a child may frighten you by behaviour that is extraordinary to you because you have never seen it before—a severe temper tantrum or a bad attack of night terrors.

You do not like to admit that you are baffled, bored or frightened, and you react by thinking there must be something wrong with you ("I'm a hopeless counselor!"), or else by blaming the child ("There must be something wrong with him!"). The truth is that your plans for dealing with such campers are frustrated, so you feel inadequate, disappointed, or angry. This is natural; there *are* children who confuse us. The important thing is that we do not act impulsively on the basis of our frustrations, but rather deal with them from our understanding of the nature of child growth and development. Your older and wiser staff members can help you with a particular child. Some general ideas about the way children grow may give you increased understanding.

Psychologists and child-study experts have been studying human development meticulously for over fifty years. You are not going to expect to become a psychologist during the summer; don't try to; indeed, to carry out your job as counselor well is far more important. It takes at least seven years to become a psychologist, and it is a mistake for you to go around using psychological terms which you have picked up. Simply attaching a tag to a child often hinders rather than helps you to understand him.

However, a few of the basic things which scientists who study human beings have discovered about children will help you understand your campers better and guide them more wisely, provided that you make a sincere attempt to consider these facts carefully and not avoid them because they seem different from your own ideas. Your director and your section head will know more about children than you do; you might discuss these ideas with them, or a psychologist or child-study specialist may be on your staff, or come to visit. Here's a wonderful chance to clarify your ideas and reach a fuller understanding.

One warning: to understand human beings is never simple; to try to over-simplify a complex matter is tempting but dangerous. If you ever think you have reached a full understanding of human beings, you deceive yourself; you have probably picked up some little gadgety formula that obscures rather than illuminates the real issues. No one knows all the answers, not even your director! And psychologists have a tremendous amount yet to learn. It is the desire to understand more fully that is vital, not the knowledge; the search (and re-search) is the essence of adventure, discovery only a part in it.

UNDERSTANDING IMMATURITY

Children are in the process of growing up; they are at different points on the trail towards maturity; they are all growing towards it but are doing so in different ways and at different rates. They have not caught up to you.

You, if you are a young counselor, have been doing some quick growing up yourself. In taking a camp job you have accepted adult responsibility; you try to think as an adult, speak as an adult, behave as an adult, and take on adult things. As adults we judge children often by our standards; we expect them to be more like us than like themselves. We are impatient with them if they are not; we are irked by their immaturities, forgetting that these are what they should and must show at their age and with their experience.

A child must be childish. If he were not immature he would be psychologically or physiologically a freak. St. Paul stated this when he said, "When I was a child, I spake as a child, I understood as a child, I thought as a child." Such childish ways are obviously immature ways of thinking and acting; but they are in no sense undesirable ways. Indeed they are natural, and highly desirable.

Children at different ages are of course at very different

points along the road to maturity. The fifteen-year-olds have had three times as much living as the fives. There is greater difference between them than there is between twenty- and sixty-year-olds! It is to be hoped that you are with an age group with whose immaturities you feel comfortable. If you are annoyed by the "childishness" of five-year-olds, who insist on playing in the sand when you want them to learn to paddle, or if you are disgusted with a wet bed, or irked by a child's inability to keep his mind on getting dressed, perhaps you could be moved to another age group. If you are supervising fourteen-year-olds and find that you are bothered by their immaturities of horsing around, having a definite opinion on everything, using colourful slang, talking too much of sex, cars and crime, and having a tendency to practical jokes, perhaps you could be moved to look after a younger group.

One important factor in understanding children of any age is to anticipate as much as you can, but never be surprised at anything. You will find children behave in ways you consider inadequate ("He can't even make his own bed"), naughty ("She wiggles so much at the table"), ornery ("They simply don't remember what I tell them"). But if you understand that these are all normal phases of the normal child, such understanding should enable you partly to anticipate and certainly to accept.

As they grow towards maturity, the things children put first are not the ones you do. Cleanliness, politeness, being considerate, working at a skill with extended concentration, are important to you; they are not to children. You and your camp think it frightfully important that everyone be on time; children have little sense of time. They are not overly concerned with the fact that raincoats keep the rain off; however, if they get wet and cold, they want to be dry and warm immediately and want someone to see that they are.

Children are not able to do things well, certainly not as

well as you. Why should they be? They have lots of time to learn. So why be impatient if they can't tie their shoes, control their elimination, eat with highly polished manners, use a paddle properly, know the words of the camp songs, or stay awake at an evening program? If they could do all these things, they would not be children or campers; they would be adults. In due time they will be adults and act as adults.

Too, children are prone to feel quick emotion and to express it. If they are sad or frightened or lonely, they may cry. It's no use saying, "Boys don't cry." For as one replied, "That's a lie. I'm a boy, and I'm crying." One sign of your own maturity is the ease with which you can tolerate tears, accepting them without embarrassment as a cry for help. You will also meet sudden anger, temper tantrums, outbursts of indignation—"You did, you did, you did, you are a cruel, bad meanie!" And there will be unexpected moods, sulkiness, the cause of which you do not know and cannot discover.

Then there will be fears—fear of water, of the dark, of going on an errand alone, of the noise in the dining-room, of supposed desertion by parents, of the director or a handyman or a boisterous counselor. Though you may never have felt these fears yourself, it will be unfortunate if they seem just silly to you, for they are not silly to the child; they are very real. You may see a child in panic; perhaps he has been forced into doing something he is deeply afraid of. This may frighten you; do not be surprised at either his panic or your own fear. These things are natural in the process of growing up. If we think children should be like adults they will irritate or confuse us; we make our first real step towards understanding when we realize that immaturities are necessary stages in the process of growing up.

Because we are prone to give more attention to childish qualities that disturb or irritate us, we forget the delightful qualities that children have. These too are part of their immaturity, and are often unfortunately lost in adulthood.

Children have a deep curiosity and interest in the world, for it is still new and intriguing to them. Things around them—not, by any means, always the things we think they should attend to—make them want to stop, look, and listen. They ask questions about what, why, when, and how; and if we are not too busy telling them what we think they should know, we can listen and encourage them on their wondering quest. Every child is something of a scientist in that he wants to learn, to know about things that catch his interest. His interest may be fleeting rather than sustained, but how much more refreshing his outlook is than the taking-things-for-granted attitude of so many adults!

Then, too, children have an emotional genuineness and honesty, free from ulterior motives. This may be reflected in impulsiveness, which should not embarrass you. If a child likes or does not like something or someone, he expresses his true feeling, rather than saying what is conventionally acceptable. He may throw his arms around you if he is delighted. He may state rather loudly that a distinguished visitor looks rather like a fish—which is perhaps true. He may write a poem describing his exact feelings—"I heard a bee go buzz, buzz, buzz, So I ran away from where he was"—or paint a picture of the camp director which in your opinion resembles a pile-driver more than a person.

At times you will be astonished by the thoughtfulness of children for one another: "Johnny feels badly because his mother didn't get him a knife; let's all put in some money and get him one." At other times you will be amazed by their shrewd insights into what's going on: "The director wants us all to be in our best clothes and sing our nicest songs, so he can get money from those visitors for the new lodge". You will be made glad by their imagination, by their seriousness, by their uncontrolled delight, and by their amazing acceptance and tolerance of you.

Can you help children retain some of these good qualities,

which the world so quickly stamps out? As grown-ups we have learned not only to control the expression of our real experience, but to deny that it exists. In attaining self-control we have become psychologically dishonest. Denying our fears and angers, likes and dislikes, does not dissipate them; it distorts them. As adults we often have to fool other people about our feelings; it is a pity that we fool ourselves. Indeed, in growing up we all too often put away the *wrong* childish things. We lose the child's belief in the world as he sees, touches, and feels it; we doubt our own feelings and experiences. As St. Paul might have added, "When I was a child, I felt as a child; now I have become a man, I feel as *They* tell me I should."

ANTICIPATION AND EXPECTATION

So you realize that the first step towards understanding your campers is that you accept this idea of phases of immaturity; you are going not only to tolerate, but to appreciate, a child's being a child; you are no longer trying to push children into maturity, nor are you disturbed because they are not hurrying to become adults. The next question is: how are you going to deal with children at these various phases of immaturity? There are two important strategies: *anticipation* and *expectation*.

You can learn something about what children at a certain age level are generally like. Your camp director, your psychologist, and many books available from the city or camp library can help you here. Beyond these, you can quickly pick up cues from your first few days of living with the campers themselves. From all this you can anticipate what may happen and plan properly for it. You anticipate that your young group is not going to make much progress in tidying up. Therefore you plan not merely to supervise but to do a good deal of the job yourself. Johnny never remembers his rubbers; you see that he puts them on. You plan times in the day when things that have to be done are done. You will often have to remind; but never nag. You be the clock for them, and say, "It's time to go to dinner now. Let's go."

George leaves his paddle on the beach when he is dashing off to something; why not get it and put it away for him this time? When children fail it is usually because we are asking too much of them. We have anticipated too much. When Linda refuses to join the swimming class, you might well plan to spend time with her by the water's edge, getting her to feel and touch the water and grow acquainted with it.

Is there no time for tears? There should be. You should anticipate that there will be tears. The child needs something, probably you. Plan to take him where he can be quiet, and let him cry. Stay with him if he wants you to. Do not apologize for him. You probably cry at times, and even the camp director would like to. When the spasm is over, you may be told what the matter was, or you may not. Don't pry; try to infer.

In dealing with temper, the main thing is that you remain calm yourself, take the child away from the anger-provoking situation, let anger run its course, and when he is ready, let him return to the group. Plan a time later on to discuss emotional upsets with him, but don't let him feel that they are unnatural or make him different from the others.

Your second strategy is that of *expectation*. You are not going to expect that by tomorrow the child will act as an adult, but you should expect that by tomorrow he will be one small step ahead of today. One expects an adult to make a bed efficiently—smooth sheets, tight corners, tidy surface. Your camper does not make his at all; your expectation is that tomorrow he will help you put on one sheet. If you aim at his achieving your own top performance, you will defeat your purpose. He will be discouraged and so will you.

If Susy wiggles and fidgets all through the meal and flicks

little crumbs, see if she can try sitting quietly for two minutes, then let her get up to pass or fetch something. If Bobby cries every time something goes wrong, he does it because he wants help and finds that tears bring you to his aid. So tell him that when he feels like crying, all he has to do is call you and you'll be there. Your expectation is that gradually there will be no need for tears.

If some older campers insist on using a very limited and tedious vocabulary of slang and vying with each other in pithy pieces of profanity, assure them that they are not being very clever, that most adults, including yourself, know all these words and that there are better ones to express your meaning. Looking up *damn* in the dictionary usually convinces one that it is not exactly the right word to convey what one really means. Your expectation is that the camper will try to be a bit more capable in communicating than he is being.

And so your strategies are to *anticipate* what the campers will do and plan for it to be taken care of, and to *expect* that their progress will be one small step ahead. Maturity is attained by the accumulation of these small steps in the right direction, not by a great big jump. Remember it takes time to grow and the process can be so very pleasant. We adults have a bad fault; we can hardly see a child without wanting to push and hurry him up. We should be as thrilled as he is with the one little step forward.

Going Backwards

Some days the steps will go backwards. The campers who had made great headway in tidiness now leave their cabin a total mess. The boy who controlled his crying for days has a terrific outburst. You may be disappointed, but there is no need to be. Psychologists call these occurrences regressions (going backwards), and we all have them. They often occur when much—perhaps too much—effort has been put into achieving. In such circumstances all of us tire, our feet slip, and we fall back to an earlier stage of development and use a device that worked then. Don't be alarmed, don't be angry, and don't let anyone feel ashamed. Just go on, perhaps a little more slowly at first. Your wonderful reassurance is that in the long run most children can't help growing up. They do become more efficient, more organized, more responsible, more controlled. Of course, if a child stays at the place to which he slipped back, and fails to move forward again, you had better talk to someone more experienced than yourself. Sustained (fixated) regressions need expert help, for they can become real blocks to growing up.

A very natural regression which most of us experience at times is homesickness. Even as adults we sometimes look back with nostalgia to the safety, warmth, and security of our childhood homes. The strangeness and newness of camp may frighten some child and make him want to escape from it all and go home to the safety he had found at an earlier stage. The extraordinary thing is that it is often children who feel least safe and sure in their homes who show most homesickness. Perhaps their very uncertainty makes them feel that home may vanish or their parents forget them while they are away. Children who are happy about, and sure of, their homes rarely become homesick except for fleeting moments that quickly disappear.

Your camp director will have his own suggestions for dealing with homesickness and will give you help with a deeply homesick child. One good plan some camp directors follow is to advise you to agree with the child who wants to go home, and tell him that of course he can go if he still wants to in a few days' time; then begin to look up transportation schedules. If the child believes you really mean it, he will feel very much better. For once we are certain we can escape from an uncomfortable situation, we can tolerate it, and even begin to enjoy it. During these few days the child will need a great deal of your support, and you will find things *he* is really interested in and help him become involved in them. He may forget all about wanting to go home. If at the end of the time he holds you to your agreement, then of course you have to let him go. He will possibly change his mind when he actually gets to the bus, and come back with you. If he does not, don't be disappointed. He may not have sufficient "camp readiness." By next year we hope that he will.

So you now realize that every child is at his own particular place along his way towards maturity, and that children differ in the paths they take towards it. You realize that your job is to accept their immaturities, to help them make small steps forward and not to be disappointed when they slip back. But the trail towards maturity is an upward one and progress requires an effort. We know that effort requires strength, so now let us consider the sources from which such strength comes.

STRENGTHS FOR GROWING UP

During recent years doctors and psychologists who have been studying babies and young children have made a surprising discovery. Babies in some institutions do not grow in human qualities. In spite of good food, clean surroundings, and efficient physical care, these children are psychologically stunted. They become apathetic, make no effort, and cannot even play. What they lack are close intimate personal relationships with adults. They are deprived of the intimate care, affection, and interest of parents or other adults. Many become more and more feeble, not only psychologically but physically. Some, despite proper food and warmth, even die. However, if the damage is not too great, when these young children are placed with loving, interested foster-parents, there is often a remarkable improvement.

Studies of such babies in institutions, as well as of children in homes which lack good relationships between adults and children, have taught us that the primary source of strength for growing towards maturity comes from the personal care and respect of adults. Through his secure feeling of relationship with adults, a child develops a sense of trust and faith in them, and from this a feeling that he is all right and that life is going to be all right.

TRUST IN ADULTS

The most important relationships a child has are those with his parents. A child who through infancy and the early years has developed a feeling of trust in his parents will believe in the goodness and support of other adults—including you. We call such children mentally well. They will accept you and expect that you have much to offer.

However, children for whom this primary relationship has been lacking or unsatisfactory will grow up doubting, disliking, and even despising grown-ups, including you. Their deep distrust, their conviction that adults are against them rather than for them, their anger towards adults for hurts they have received, and their fear of feeling a glimmer of trust in anyone lest they may again be let down, may show up directly. Most likely it will not; rather it will be reflected in behaviour which you consider odd or undesirable and which it is of little use to try to correct by superficial measures.

Many children, of course, will show odd behaviour at first because camp is strange to them, and some will be sitting on the fence, waiting to see what camp adults are like. If in the ordinary course of camp life these things do not improve, you may guess that previous relationships the child has had with adults have been weak, and you will do what you can to establish and strengthen good relationships with him. For example, a child who over-conforms, is overly polite, who always does exactly as he is supposed to without argument but without much interest, may behave this way because he is thoroughly frightened of what adults would do to him if he were more conspicuous. Also, a camper who is belligerent and aggressive and against all rules and regulations just for the sake of being so, may unwittingly be expressing his lack of faith in adults and the world they have made for him.

The obvious but ineffectual tack we often take with such campers is to try to deal with the surface behaviour. We may just let the over-conformer be—he is such a good little boy and so easy to handle. Or we may get fed up with his obsequiousness and say, "Can't you ever make up your own mind?" or "For goodness' sake, decide for yourself!" In either case we have done nothing to increase his faith in ourselves or other adults.

Perhaps we may try harsher measures to make the aggressive camper behave—"Be really tough with him and he'll soon learn," or "Next time he takes other kids' things without asking, make him sit in the camp director's office all day." By these measures you may make some of his obvious aggressiveness disappear, but he will probably learn to express it in more subtle and dangerous forms. In any case, his faith in adults has not grown; indeed, whatever glimmers he had have probably diminished.

Camp offers the wonderful opportunity of providing a second chance for such children to develop trust in adults. To do so, camp adults (including you) must prove that they are trustworthy. This is best done if they constantly demonstrate that they are *dependable,* that they have *control* in all situations and through all vicissitudes, and that they feel *compassion.*

Dependability means that you are always for the child, not against him; that he can always turn to you for your support, your care and your help. He can count on you and he can predict what you will do. You achieve this not merely through your continual care for and interest in him, but through your truthfulness; what you say you will do, you do. This is why the matter of controls is so important. They demonstrate your dependability.

It is interesting that as he begins to trust your dependability, a camper may begin to test it—to try out the limits to which it can be stretched. Because he is beginning to believe in you, he may try you out by being particularly defiant, tiresome, rebellious and difficult. It is often at this point that an adult gives up. "I did everything for him and he was getting along so well, and now he has gone and taken money from the chapel collection; I'll never trust him again. It didn't work." But it will, if you refuse to let it fail now! Do you still accept him, can he still turn to you, do you still believe in him? Of course, you are going to see that he returns the money and make him understand that taking collection money is not to be done, but you are not going to try to accomplish this either by getting mad at him or by making him feel guilty, for by either method you weaken your dependability. You are going to do so by use of your *controls*. Remember, his main interest was not in taking the money; it was in testing your dependability.

Controls means effective ways to restrain children from doing what must not be done and to enable them to learn and to accept what should be done. You, as a counselor, want to control campers effectively. Actually, campers equally want to know that you are in control and can take charge.

Many people have difficulty in controlling children because they raise a lot of side issues, and are not clear as to what they really want to accomplish; or their difficulty may arise because they fail to think out the effective ways of accomplishing what they want to do. So when Johnny steals the money, you may shout at him, lecture him, hurt his feelings, hold him up as a public example or even whip him. Let us ask what you really want to achieve.

Certainly you do not want to make it an opportunity to express your moral indignation and smugly demonstrate your own self-righteousness, No, what you really want is (1) that he return the money—so you go with him inconspicuously to see that he does so; (2) that he refrain from taking it again; (3) that he understand and accept the purpose of collection, so you explain why the money is to be left on the plate. You tell him that if he takes it again, he will simply have to put it back again, and perhaps miss some camp activity while he is doing so.

Using this method has prevented what he really wanted—to get a rise out of you and cause a commotion in the camp. Instead, you have set up a *requirement*—collection must stay on the plate—and introduced a *consequence*—"If you do not leave it there, you miss other things and go through the boring process of returning it." Requirements and consequences are the essentials of what is meant by discipline.

Discipline is not retribution, retaliation, or punishment. Rather it is a form of teaching, a means of helping an individual learn to accept what happens when he behaves in certain ways. Discipline comes from the same root as *disciple* —a follower of a teacher.

Discipline is most effective when the child knows what the requirements are; that is what he is supposed to be trying to learn, and what the consequences will be if he does not meet them.

Requirements and consequences are pretty obvious in sports and other camp activities. You must be able to swim fifty yards, then you can go into the deeper water; if you do not learn to swim that far you stay in the shallow pool. You will note that for each requirement there are two possible consequences: what happens if you meet it, what happens if you do not. Therefore, a child always has the opportunity to make a decision and choose between the possible consequences. So when we really want him to learn something we load the dice in such a way that the consequences of meeting the requirement will be more pleasant than those of not doing so.

It is fairly easy to see how requirements and consequences work in a straightforward teaching situation, but rather more difficult in the realm of general behaviour and everyday living. However, the following principles—adapted from *The Adult and the Nursery School Child* by Margaret I. Fletcher —should be helpful in setting up a plan of discipline for your cabin group:

1. Know exactly what it is that you want children to learn.
2. Let your requirements be:
   few in number
   set up to meet necessary situations
   clearly defined
   obviously reasonable
   within the child's capacity
3. Let your consequences be:
   clear cut
   natural results of the child's actions, so that their lesson will be plain to him
   immediate, or as nearly so as possible
   proportionate to the child's stage of learning
   inevitable

Let's see how this plan will work out with your cabin group. There are a great many things you would like your campers to do: Jane to talk less, Susy to wear socks of a different colour, the group not to be so giggly. But you are not going to set up requirements about all these; you are going to let most of them go, and be patient. Suppose, however, that one thing you really want the group to do is to be quiet in rest hour. You select this as one of the *few* things about which you set up a requirement. Define clearly what you want. Do you expect complete quiet for an hour, for fifteen minutes? Or do you mean quiet activities? Get it defined so it is reasonable and within the campers' capacity. Suppose after figuring it out, probably with the help of your group, your requirement is: "Real quiet, no talking or noises or rustling paper, everybody trying to sleep, for half an hour; after half an hour, if it's not disturbing to anyone, there can be quiet talking, or writing, or reading."

Now you have to find a "teaching" consequence, that is, one that will help the children to learn to accept the requirement, not to ignore it. The consequence of meeting the requirement is of course that the child stays with his cabin group and with you. If he doesn't, what is the consequence to be? Perhaps you will decide the noisy child is to be removed elsewhere, by himself. So on the first note of noise you do just this. Certainly the consequence has to be practical, and effective for your camp, and it has to be carried out without fail.

We have used rest hour as an example of a plan of discipline which is based on requirements and consequences. Suppose you think of other situations in which you are going to use this plan of discipline for your cabin group. In each situation you consider, first, is this requirement necessary? And second, is the consequence wise, just, and practical, and one from which the campers learn?

Once children are clear as to what a requirement is and what the consequences will be, don't keep on warning and reminding; carry through immediately with what you decided would happen. Let them learn from experiencing the consequences, not from your talking about them. By doing this, children go through a real learning situation; and, more important, this increases their sense of your dependability; they know that you can be relied on to do what you say.

If you use this plan of discipline wisely, you never need get angry or emotionally involved, when a camper is not meeting the requirement; you simply follow through with the consequence. Nor does the camper get angry with you personally. He may be exasperated by the consequence, but this is something that just happens, like the weather; there is nothing personal in it. Thus your relationship with a child is never weakened by his behaviour, or by your need to control him. It remains steadfast; the plan of which you are the just administrator takes care of the matter and all goes well.

In setting up requirements you must, to some extent, play it by ear. If they are too difficult your campers cannot possibly meet them; therefore make them easier. For example, if you require six-year-olds to sit still through the whole camp concert, or else leave, they will probably all straggle out. Why not have them sit still for the first part only, and then all go out to play?

You might read these paragraphs over once a week and check what you have actually done against what they suggest, and perhaps discuss this plan in counselor's meetings and see how requirements and consequences are worked out. If you seriously work at it, you will find that not only is it effective, but it sustains what you want most to sustain—good, trusting relationships between you and the campers. If you are a young counselor, the error you are most likely to make is that of forgetting that consequences should be "teaching" consequences, not opportunities for making life tough or unpleasant or frightening for the children, or for venting your own feelings.

As well as being dependable and using effective controls, you must have *compassion*. Psychologists use the word *empathy*. Sympathy means feeling with the other person; empathy means understanding how the other person feels, although you do not feel this way yourself. You try to understand how it feels to Johnny to be a stranger in a great big camp, to Ruthie to know that despite her boasts about her beautiful home there is no one there who really cares for her, to Jimmy to believe that no matter what he does his father will never be pleased with him. If you have compassion you will never mock children for the way they feel or for the way they act under such feelings, or tell them they are silly to feel so and act so. You will accept the matters that are serious to them, and realize that their feelings and worries and hopes are as important as your concerns are to you.

So now you understand that the primary source of strength from which children make effort to move towards maturity is the trust-faith-confidence they have in adults. Adults must prove themselves trustworthy. To do so they must be dependable, maintain control, and have compassion.

SELF-TRUST

Those children who are sure of their adults are the ones who are most eager to venture out on their own. They are not afraid to do so, because, supported by their trust in adults, they have developed trust in themselves. They want to try things for themselves, to learn. Being assured of the trustworthiness of adults, they are willing to make independent effort. They show initiative, originality, and persistence. Their effort is directed to what attracts them in the world around them. Later it comes from within them through their own growing interests.

All the activities going on at camp—swimming, boating, fire-building, exploring—provide opportunities which campers who have self-trust want to use in order to find out, to learn to do better, to achieve. The camper who has developed interest in art, or in collecting natural objects, or in building things is going to pursue these activities whenever he finds a chance to do so.

There is no need whatsoever to force or to motivate well children to be active; their interests, their curiosity, and the faith they have that adults are backing them provide sufficient incentive for them to go ahead. The important things for you to do are first, to provide opportunity for their efforts, and second, to be a source of strength if things go wrong or are too difficult. If a camper with self-trust is aware of the activities that are available at camp, he will try them; if he finds other things he himself wants to do, such as making a rock collection, he will confidently go ahead unless someone or something stops him.

However, a camper's efforts may be blocked. A rock is too far away for him to bring back, or he can't quite get the knack of the stern stroke. Here, if he has trust in you, he will ask for help, or if he needs help you will offer it. He will accept your offer. Only children who lack trust in adults try to pretend that they are completely independent and want to do everything themselves. If a child's confidence in himself enables him to make efforts on his own, he still has to be willing to accept help from others, if he is really to grow towards maturity.

We have all put so much emphasis on children learning to do things on their own that we forget how important it is that they should also learn to accept help. No one can exist without other people to help him; no matter how grown up we are, we are dependent upon other people. Indeed, the more responsibility a person assumes, the more he is dependent on the help and support of others. It is too bad some children have been taught to feel that to accept help is undesirable. Actually, willingness to be helped is necessary in some circumstances, increases efficiency in others, and makes tasks more enjoyable. It is so much more fun to work with other people than completely on one's own, whether one is cooking supper at a camp-fire or writing a book. Your great contribution to campers in carrying out their activities and interests is to give them help when they need it, and support their efforts. In this way you are promoting their self-effort, and enabling them to appreciate the help and support of others.

Some system of awards will probably be used in your camp. A badge, a feather, or a bar may be given when a child has progressed to a certain point in a camp activity.

These are fun and give social recognition; but they are not the actual cause of a child's improving his swimming or archery or paddling. His improvement results from hard effort which he has put into the task; and we hope that this effort comes from the interest he has in swimming and wanting to swim better, not in wanting to get a blue cap. The fulfilment of interest is the only true basis for continuing effort. Essentially it is the achieving, not the achievement, that is important; the process, not the product, that is the fundamental reality.

No matter what system of awards your camp uses or how much emphasis it places on them, your job as the child's counselor is to support his efforts, regardless of his achievements. Your camper may not have reached the standards for a coloured swimming badge, but perhaps he has put more effort into learning to swim three strokes than the best swimmer has into getting his badge. You must realize this, and make him feel that it is the effort that is important to you. Never change your support of the camper, whether he attains a formal award or not. His formal success or failure makes no difference to your faith in him. Thus you help the child to find his satisfaction in effort towards ends important to him, and to see rewards as fringe benefits only.

Blue swimming caps and other awards are useful as official markers by which an individual's progress along certain lines can quickly be identified, and which indicate to him and other people that he is now ready to advance further. An individual is no better or worse as a person for having attained such an award. The effort he has put into it and what he learned in doing so are what really count.

Sometimes camps make too much use of awards, because they are so fashionable in our society. But provided that they are established in such a way that everyone who attains a certain level of competence receives one, they have a real value. If there are too many, given for almost everything that

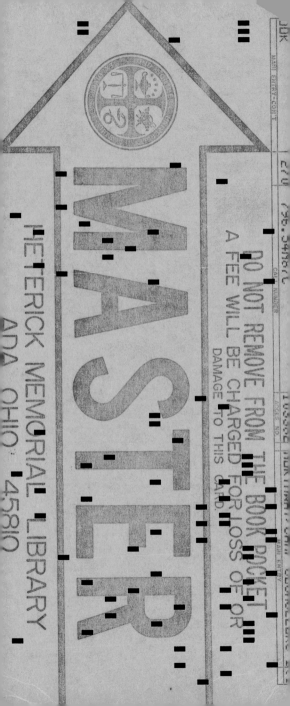

campers do, it may be that there is something lacking in the intrinsic value of the program. Perhaps campers are encouraged to work for a badge, because there are not sufficiently interesting activities or interested people to encourage effort for its own sake. You could discuss this matter with your senior staff. Certainly you can help by being more interested in your campers and by finding them interesting things to do.

Most camps agree that *competitive* awards, those that only the best two or three children can obtain, are definitely undesirable, since all the rest of the children may get the idea that they have failed. But the hazard is even more serious, for competitive awards put children in a position of vying with one another. As the third source of strength for growing towards maturity comes from one's relationships with contemporaries, it is important that we provide opportunities for co-operative experiences for campers, rather than pit them against one another.

RELATIONSHIPS WITH CONTEMPORARIES

This source of strength for a child's growing up includes his friendships with other campers and the place he fills in the group. Good relationships with contemporaries are extremely important in children's development. Although relationships with adults are primary, those with contemporaries are the persisting and final ones. The time comes in nearly everyone's life when he has no more grown-ups to lean on. Mature living depends on interaction and understanding among contemporaries. If trust in these relationships is acquired in childhood, a great many of the problems of the adult world disappear, or at least striving towards solutions for them is facilitated.

Development of relationships with contemporaries is more subtle than we used to suppose. In the last ten years psychologists have learned a great deal about it. It begins in pre-school years. The sequence is as follows:

1. The child has good relationships with his adults. He finds them trustworthy and knows that they will support and encourage him. (*Dependence*)
2. From this he develops self-trust, out of which he ventures forth and develops interests. In doing so, he becomes interesting. (*Independence*)
3. The starting-point for his relationship with other children is that he finds that things they do are interesting to him, and things he does are interesting to them. (*Inter-independence*)
4. Out of association on the basis of intertwined interests, gradually as a child grows up some of the support he first received from his parents now comes from his contemporaries; but he also offers *them* support and dependence such as they received from their parents. (*Mature interdependence*)

If you understand this sequence, you will realize that the first reason why children associate with one another is because they have interests and are interesting to one another. Only very slowly does the relationship grow to include mutual dependence and support. Children cannot be to other children a reliable base of trustworthiness; this takes years of learning, so do not expect too much too soon.

You should also understand that this sequence is like a stairway. If a child is really having a difficult time making friends or becoming part of the group, you have to help him by letting him go one or two steps back. He needs more trust in adults and in himself before he is capable of forming good relationships with contemporaries.

Because contemporary relationships are so important, your job is to see that for your campers they are pleasant rather than unpleasant, enhancing rather than frustrating, encouraging rather than frightening. So you will do two things: *plan* and *produce*.

In *planning* for campers' experiences with one another, you will realize that children have not learned to control their own feelings, nor have they acquired the skills to deal with complicated or lengthy social situations. They can quickly become irked with one another and express their feelings by being terribly mean. They often go into a tizzy or begin to quarrel over matters that seem trivial to you. Jimmy takes Bill's flashlight and doesn't put it back, and Billy gets mad.

You can prevent much of this unpleasantness by planning: separate places for possessions, and requirements about their use; constructive things to do together centred around common interests; opportunities to be away from one another with other groups; and, above all—and this is often the hardest to work out in camps—time for a camper to be alone. Children suffer from social fatigue even more than they do from physical fatigue. They need time to themselves to pursue their own interests, or even just to sit and look and dream. Adults have a terrible urge to push them continually to be one of the gang, to participate in activities, to do what the others do. Resist this urge; a child should never be forced to join in. It is his privilege to be on his own.

You must also *produce* an atmosphere through which campers learn to appreciate the fact that each of them has his unique assets and liabilities, strengths and weaknesses, and that when these are wisely combined, the group as a whole has enriched experiences. Joe is slow in picking up ideas, but will do more than his share in tidying the cabin. Billy is very shy in public, but oh how he can play the trumpet! Martin can tell funny stories in front of the whole camp but is weak in carrying packs over portages. If you capitalize on the strengths of each rather than trying to make everyone share equally in everything, your campers will learn to accept each other's differences; they will discover that it is by using the variety of assets which each can contribute that social living becomes worth while. Actually it is the variety of personalities that gives social life its colour and its challenge. If everyone were the same—even if they were all like you, like me, or like the camp director—what a very dull world this would be!

From studies,* made during the last ten years, of children's relationships with one another, two facts have been found which have importance for you.

First, children differ in their *social potential,* and their level remains remarkably constant over a period of several years. This means that some children have more social energy, more outgoingness, than others. They make acquaintances easily, enjoy social activities, assume leadership, and are widely known. Others are much less conspicuous in the group, do not make many social contacts, are hesitant about entering social situations. You will have campers of different social potential in your group, and you may have talked about this difference in their popularity. Your inclination very likely is to try to help all your campers to become more popular.

Our advice to you is, don't. Regard these differences as you would differences in intelligence or in physical strength, and do not try to change them.

Many of us are indocrinated by the North American assumption that high popularity and conspicuousness in a group are inherently good things. This is simply not true. In fact, research has shown that individuals who are around

*These studies were carried out at the Institute of Child Study, University of Toronto, with financial support of the Canadian Government under health grants. Nos. 605-5: 147; 288; 312. The results have been given in various publications; two which would be of most interest to camp counselors are Northway and Weld, *Sociometric Testing: A Guide for Teachers;* and Northway, *What Is Popularity?*

the average in social potential and have one or two intimate friends are best off from the standpoint of mental health.

Your real job is not to try to push children towards being highly popular, or make them feel bad for not having more friends. Rather your contribution is to help them strengthen the social relationships they are forming, and use their varieties of social ability constructively as part of the group. Who is to say which camper contributes most in the long run—the flamboyant character with a pack of ideas, or the quiet youngster who pursues his group responsibilities? the child who is always elected a team captain, or the one who paints pictures? the camper who is a friend to everyone, or the one who is trustworthy in his few close relationships? Help them to live at their own social potential and to work out their own social patterns, to feel a value in their unique part in the social world rather than to envy some ideal image of the social personality that they or you think they should be.

In the cabin group you will find many ways of using the social differences of your campers. Do not try to fit them into one mould. This is like making everyone wear the same size suit; there are bound to be misfits. However, there are children whose relationships with contemporaries are such that they do need help. These are, first, the isolated child who, over a period of time, has literally no friends at all; second, the child who is very highly popular and conspicuous in camp affairs, but who lacks intimate friends and is badly upset if he loses his leadership in any situation. For these campers your best action is to consult your more experienced camp staff members and follow the advice they give you.

Second, there is the fact of *preference.* All human beings prefer to associate with some people rather than with others. This is true of your campers as it is true of you. See that campers have plenty of time to be with those they like to be with. A camper knows better than you do whom he feels most friendly towards, and it is in these naturally congenial relationships that personality grows.

There are some facts about human preferences that you should know:

(a) *There is no one who is preferred by everybody.* Even the most popular camper has people who are indifferent to him; some may even dislike him. Help your campers accept the fact that it is impossible to be universally liked, and that to strive to do so is foolish. Better to sit back and relax and rejoice in the fact that they are liked by some and held in real affection and regard by others.

(b) *Nearly everyone is preferred by some.* It is rare indeed to find a camper whom no one likes at all. If you look carefully, you will find that even the quiet one who you think has no friends chums up with someone for something. Foster these fragile bonds, and from them stronger relationships will grow.

(c) *Preferences exist between adults and children.* Do not be surprised if some of your campers do not like you as much as others do, and accept quite honestly the fact that you prefer some of them to others. You will of course respect, be interested in, and be fair and just to all of them; but you will intuitively like some more than others. It is probably where there is a mutual liking between a child and an adult that the adult can be of greatest help in fostering the child's growing up.

Camp is a wonderful place for developing good contemporary relationships, for fostering inter-independence and mature interdependence. Through friendships and by their feeling of having their unique significance in the group, children develop trust, faith and confidence in their contemporary world; and as they do, they truly progress towards maturity.

Now that you have read this chapter, you have a great many ideas to think about. Discuss them with your superiors and your fellow counselors, and go ahead and read other books which will help explain them.

We have given you two main ideas: first, that growing up means passing through steps along the trail towards maturity; second, that the strengths to make the effort of going forward come out of one's trust in adults, trust in oneself, and trust in contemporaries. These ideas will, we hope, help you to understand your campers better. They may also help you to understand yourself. For you too are in the process of growing towards maturity; so is your camp director; so are the writers of this book. For maturity is an ever receding goal. It is the attaining, not the attainment, that is the reality.

As W. E. Blatz wrote in *Hostages to Peace:* "Life is a continuous process and there is no one goal other than the desire to go further which can satisfy an individual. . . . Life is not fulfilment, but fulfilling. . . . A complete life is never finished."

Chapter Three

YOU AND YOUR CABIN GROUP

Margaret Govan

YOUR key job as a counselor will be to look after a cabin or tent group of four to eight campers. These youngsters will be your special charges and the cabin will be their home within the camp. With you as the adult to care for and about them, instead of their mothers and fathers, you make up a camp "family."

The amount of responsibility you will be expected to take and the time you are required to spend with these campers differ in various camps. It is almost certain you will start and end the day with them, probably have some meals with them, and plan for their free time and cabin-group projects. You may be expected to attend activity classes with them or even to take them on out-of-camp trips. However, no matter how much or how little of the day you are together, these campers are especially yours. You will grow to know them pretty well; you will look after the details of their care, from choosing proper clothing to participating in camp programs; and you will try to help them grow in happy relationships within this "home" group.

BEFORE THE CAMPERS COME

As the opening day approaches you may suffer from certain qualms. What will your group be like? Will they present problems beyond your capabilities, or will you be equal to the job? Will the campers like you? Will you like them?

Learn your campers' names. In addition, learn all that you can about them from the director or your supervisor. The more you know about a child, his background, interests, dislikes, fears, skills, and handicaps, the better you can understand him. Do not pay much attention to what counselors tell you about him as he was last year. He is older now and different. Start him off with a clean slate and form your own opinion.

It is important to know which of your campers are old and which new, in what grades they are in school, where they come from, and, of course, their ages. The campers will be somewhat like you were when you were the same age. You may remember something of what it was like to be seven or ten or fifteen. Most of them will have small problems with growing up, as you had. Most of them will expect to like you, but at the same time they will be curious to see what you are like, and they will try to find out. And you will remember that they are individuals, just as you are, with their own likes and dislikes, needs and dreams. They will respond to friendly interest and consideration. You are older—quite old, in their estimation—and should be more tolerant, more objective than they are. Be prepared to accept the camper who is the least like you remember being, as well as the one who appears to be a reflection of your young self.

You will want to think about your goals for your campers individually and the cabin group as a whole, and relate these to the over-all goals of your camp. Your goals will be set up in the light of the campers' ages and experience, and the parents' expectations.

Of course you will want your charges to be healthy and safe, to learn new skills and improve old ones. You will want the cabin members to become a group, planning, carrying out plans, evaluating, learning to work together towards a purpose and to enjoy each other. You will help them find ways to achieve their goals. You will want each camper to learn how to contribute to the group, and to accept other people's contributions; to be a leader at times and a follower at other times; to learn to appreciate the things of the spirit as well as physical prowess; to learn something about independence and interdependence, law and order and self-discipline. And to have fun and lots of it. Talk to your section head or director about all this, but do not make a hard-and-fast plan of action; that can develop only as you get to know your campers.

You may be one of the official party travelling to camp with the children. If you see old pals greeting each other fondly and you know hardly anyone, you quite likely will feel as shy and lonely as the youngest new boy. Two things will help. The camp will have sent you exact instructions as to what your duties are; do them. Also (and it may be for the first time in your life), you are looked upon by the children as an adult. Act like one, forget your own qualms, talk to the stranger, sit by a new fellow, chat with any of them—they expect it. Soon after you arrive in camp, you will be briefed by your section head with necessary information. You will soon feel at home.

However, you may be at camp before the campers come. If so, see the cabin where your group is going to live, note its facilities and form some idea as to how they can best be used and shared. Also be sure you know the geography of the camp, the locations of the dining-room, lodge, and office, and especially of the toilets and washrooms. The camp director will have given you important instructions about storage of trunks, care of keys, medical supplies, campers' money. You will know about mealtimes, signal bells, and of course regulations regarding boats and swimming. You will have all this information ready to answer your campers' questions; and the more know-how you have, the more confident you will feel.

It is not enough merely to know all these things; you must understand them so that you can interpret them to the campers. For instance, if you simply take a child's pills and money to put in safekeeping, he may think that he has been robbed and that he will never see his valuables again.

THE FIRST DAY

The campers will be arriving at any moment! No matter how you may be feeling, create a pleasant welcome. Call your campers by name and attach the right name to the right face. Find out what the child is actually called, not just the name on the application. Billy may not know who you mean, if you greet him as "William Arthur." Be right there when the campers arrive; help them to settle into the cabin or tent; answer their questions about routines; show them around. And as you are doing these things, remember that they are people. Johnnie, in that hard shell, may be terribly homesick; Peter, aggressive, may be trying to hide his fear of the others; Joan, showing off, attempting to make a place for herself in the group.

Try to recollect your own feelings on your first day of camp; but do more than that—try to broaden your outlook to take in the feelings of every member of the cabin group, although some will be very unlike yours. Perhaps because of your uncertainty you will be inclined to be bossy, to push people around and show off. This is not unusual, but the more you know about what you are doing, the more calm and efficient you will be.

If the first few hours of camp life are friendly, pleasant and filled with expectations of fun and adventure, you are off to a good start. Now is the time to think about the relationships of campers to campers, and to you. Perhaps there are friends in the cabin, or they all may be friends from last year. More likely there will be both old friends, and new-comers who are strangers, and their only unifying links are the roof over their heads and *you*. (And the roof is not going to do much about it!) That is how important you are. But this situation is one which you are going to change if you possibly can. All your campers should become integrated into one group in which each has a real part, and you act as the catalyst which facilitates this.

Your first step towards developing a group feeling con-sists in settling into your new home, the cabin which you share. This requires work; but work done as a group in a happy atmosphere, is a step towards unity, and both you and the campers will know each other much better after this experience. The bed arrangement, if there is any room to arrange beds in a different way, must be done so as to keep them all in the group—no one must be stuck off to one side. Perhaps there are boxes available for use as dressing-tables, or the cabin may have shelves which have to be assigned, or shelves can be made in due course by the group. A line for bathing-suits and towels is needed too. Campers may have lockers, or in some camps trunks will be used instead. All clothes have to be checked, compared with lists, and examined for name tapes. Essentials should be left readily available and everything else carefully put away. Places for one's own pos-sessions give a feeling of at-homeness. It is always a comfort to know exactly where to find one's toothbrush. This prelim-inary settling in will depend upon when the campers arrive, and on the camp program. Also upon the weather! A violent thunderstorm or a very cold day makes a vast difference in your procedure.

One of the facts you may as well face is that on arrival at least one of your group will have lost something, often his most valued possession, and another will take violent excep-tion to the presence of bugs. Reassure the loser that you will track down the lost article, and protect the bug-worrier by having a good anti-mosquito lotion available for immediate use.

SPECIAL ACTIVITIES OF THE CABIN GROUP

An excellent way of creating cabin unity is to do something apart from the rest of camp, something a little out of the ordinary and fun for everybody in the group. This could be an exploratory hike, an adventure, a meal out, a cabin camp-fire, or a craft project. If it has an emotional significance— satisfaction in a project well carried out, appreciation of the beauty of a camp-fire or of a sunset, the enjoyment of a day on the lake, fun and laughter in which all can join, harmon-ious feelings shared, or a secret which belongs to the group alone—then so much the better.

Once a decision has been made to undertake a project, such as a cook-out, take a pencil and paper and put down all the details: how far? how long? where? when? what equip-ment? what food? Jot down every single thing, even to matches. The first few projects *must* be successful. If they are not, no matter who is to blame, the counselor loses face and the group becomes discouraged and disgruntled. All the necessities must be on hand, the project must not be too big to handle, or the distance too great for enjoyment; and you must have complete confidence that you can guide the pro-ject without any guess-work or experimentation. The time for trying out a new recipe will come later!

If you are responsible for large blocks of free time, there should be constructive ideas for it. Where do these ideas come from? Some may come from members of the group. Often their suggestions will be the result of successful projects they have carried out before, either at camp or elsewhere. Occasionally there will be a wild dreamer who has notions far beyond the strength and ability of the group. Ideas need to be sorted out, limited to the age and interests and attention span of the campers. If there are no ideas, you may try a brain-storming session. Still nothing? Then you have to put forth a couple of tentative suggestions yourself and see how they are received.

There may be a camper who always wants to do something different. Perhaps he has different interests; in this case a compromise can be made. "You come with us today; we'll go with you tomorrow." Or perhaps he will have to go with another group occasionally in order to fulfil his needs. Or again, if he is a young biologist or botanist, perhaps his interests can be worked into the project. There may be another boy who refuses to co-operate, in order to gain in importance; he wishes to be a leader and to have his ideas followed. It may be possible to find something that is so interesting that he is glad to go along with the others; or if he has a good idea, arrange to carry it out on another day. The section director would be a good person to consult at this point.

Whatever the project, you should expect to reach certain goals, in keeping with the long-range plans which you have been reconsidering since you became acquainted with your cabin group. The campers want to have fun, to learn new skills, to complete projects successfully, and to have something to talk about afterwards. In addition, you will want them to develop as individuals and as a group. Further, you will want to vary the type of project so that different interests and skills are brought in, providing new challenges and satisfying every camper's needs.

As the campers develop ability in suggesting and planning projects, you will try to get them to relate plans to needs.

"You are going out on a canoe trip later; suppose we work in some practice paddling and learn how to cook a decent meal."

"Let's go and clear the portage for ourselves and the rest of the camp."

"It's been a strenuous week; what can we do that'll give us a rest?"

And then one day you ask for suggestions and you draw a blank. You've used up all your own good ideas, too. This is where the section head or experienced counselors can give a helping hand. Or you might go to the camp library and do some idea chasing. Or could the plan of the last successful outing be sufficiently changed as to goal, or time of day, to make it entirely different?

INDIVIDUALS AND THE GROUP

You will not always be dealing with the group as a whole. At times your function is to be with individual campers. Perhaps it will be just to listen, for the value of a good listener is inestimable. Children have very little opportunity to talk, these days; homes are busy and preoccupied places. Perhaps Alan never has had an audience. And as he talks you get to know him so much better. Besides, he can often talk about his own problems and express his interests.

Or perhaps there has been trouble. Few campers can manage a two-week period without getting into some upsets with others, and you can provide a willing ear, or a shoulder to cry on, or a few words to straighten out some crooked thinking; or you can start a discussion to find out exactly what the difficulty is and what is the best solution. Sometimes encouragement is what is needed.

Too, there is the camper who needs you more than the others in the cabin. Perhaps it takes him longer to find himself as a person in camp; perhaps he's an odd child, or he hasn't had the attention that he needs in his own family. You can be a tower of strength; and the day that you discover that your support is no longer so important should be one of the most satisfying in your career. You cannot be drawn equally towards all the campers, but you can give them all thoughtful concern.

OTHER CABIN MATTERS

Your camp will have a policy regarding food being sent to campers. Camps differ a good deal. Be sure that you know what your camp's is, support it, and be able to explain it to your campers.

One of the campers has a birthday. Probably there is a traditional way of celebrating. If not, you might suggest that the other campers make little presents at the craft shop, and then as a cabin group, hold a camp-fire. If another camper has a birthday, some equally exciting celebration will be held for him too.

For ideas on what to do when it rains and how your campers can become even more of a group, see Chapter VII. Just remember that there is no harm in getting wet, only in staying wet. As soon as the dampening activity is over, change into dry, warm clothes. Heavy socks and a warm sweater are most important. If a fireplace or stove is available, gather around it and hang wet clothing to dry. A hot drink at such times works miracles.

Discipline, which is often a worrisome matter to the would-be counselor, is not as difficult a matter as you think. Your camp director will describe the kind of discipline he expects and what the rules and regulations are. He will discuss ways which he has found are effective in obtaining good discipline; and in Chapter II you will find an outline of a plan of discipline which has been found to work extremely well.

Be alert for warnings of trouble; crankiness, listlessness, boredom, sullenness, are all signs, and you must take time to read them. Often tiredness, over-tension, or worry about a test will lead to discipline problems. Sometimes there is a child who wants to know how far he can go, and takes steps to see for himself; or even a group may do this. But if you are aware of the mood of your group, you should try to analyze the reasons for it, and take action before the crisis arises.

As the general camp life goes along, something will happen to your cabin group; they will begin to act more naturally as individuals, and to show a united front to the rest of camp. Any problems there may be will come out of hiding. So will natural leadership and other characteristics. As camp days move on, you should continue to work with the group in close consultation with the section head. You interpret the group to the section head and the other counselors who are or will be involved with your group; you interpret camp to the campers.

VISITORS' DAY

Don't let visitors' day frighten you. Treat it as an opportunity to understand your campers better by meeting their parents. Remember that you share one thing in common with the parents, the overriding concern for the happiness and wellbeing of their children. Here are a few suggestions to help make your day go smoothly.

Stay near your tent or cabin until you have met the parents of all your campers, so that you can be found when there is someone to be introduced to you. Have your best foot forward. Greet them in a friendly, direct and courteous manner and with a warm smile.

Be tactful and diplomatic in your discussions. If there is some deeper problem to discuss with a parent, clear it through your unit head or the director. Be positive and be charitable. Try to find something commendable to talk about, stress the children's good points, their improvements and achievements. You must be sincere, without gushing over a parent or a camper. You cannot fool either of them for long.

Your job is to create confidence in the camp administration and leadership. If parents criticize some aspect of the camp, do not get into an argument. Accept the criticism gracefully and assure the parent that you will either attend to the matter, look into it further, or draw it to the attention of the director. Then be sure that you do it.

Try to share your time equitably between all the parents. Don't get cornered and monopolized by any one or two. When parents are about to leave and after they have left, be alert for signs of homesickness, for this is a vulnerable time. Stay close to your cabin group and keep them happily occupied, with no chance to brood. Spend extra time with them at bedtime.

THE END OF THE SEASON

And then one day you realize that camp is near the end. There are a great many things for you and your group to do. These will be easier than the things you had to do at the beginning of camp, for you all know one another and there will be time to study the instructions which your group will be given.

All possessions of the campers should be sent home clean, and packed as neatly as possible. These items should be checked with the list on the child's trunk, and lost articles should be found. At some camps worn clothing and toys for which the camper will have no further use are left in baskets for local charitable organizations. This is a good idea, as some of the child's possessions will be worn or outgrown; but you should make certain that nothing is left which the parents might think should have been returned, or that the camper wants to take.

The cabin should be left as neat at the end of camp as it was at the beginning. All items borrowed from the camp—library books, blankets, cutlery—should be returned.

The campers may not realize it, but when they return home feeling they had a thoroughly happy summer, a great deal of this happiness results from the fact that they have lived in a comfortable and orderly environment in which no detail was too small for consideration, and in which you helped them not only to organize themselves but to discover the good fellowship of being part of a united group.

Chapter Four

SAFETY AND HEALTH

Mary L. Northway & Barry G. Lowes

EVERY parent wants his child to be safe and well. Camp directors make careful, detailed plans for health and safety. These can be fully effective only with your understanding and co-operation.

In every camp there are regulations and requirements designed to promote health and safety. Some of these are established by the law—federal, provincial or state, and local. Others are set forth by camping associations and organizations in their statements on "standards and desirable camping practices." Still others are worked out by your own camp to meet its particular needs and situation. You should know the regulations and requirements for health and safety of your camp, for you will be the person who has to see that they are carried out. This chapter describes some important aspects of health and safety. Discuss how they apply to your camp and learn from your director other measures which he considers important.

SAFETY

The two potential hazards at camp are accidents and fire. Prevention of both of these should be your primary aim.

This chapter is based on the following contributions to *Charting the Counselor's Course* (Longmans, 1940, now out of print): "Keeping Campers Well" by Dorothy M. James, and "Safety in Camp" by Dorothy N. R. Jackson.

The newer camp buildings are being constructed to reduce the chance of fire, and the waterfront and other play areas are increasingly being designed to minimize the possibility of accident.

The waterfront in many camps is not only the most vital activity area, but the one offering the most complex and varied safety problems. The site determines the type of dock, the sort of boats, and the necessary protection. The swimming area should be clearly marked and limited, free from sunken logs and other underwater hazards, and should include a defined shallow pool or section of protected water. The swimming dock should be separate from the boating area. The floats and docks should be checked frequently for split or loose boards, or unsafe ladders.

Regulations for counselors' and visitors' swimming and boating will be made clear to you, so that you will know when, where, and under what conditions you may swim or use boats, and will be able to convey tactfully to visitors what the regulations are. Whether you are a waterfront counselor or not, you may be called upon from time to time to participate in safety patrols or serve as an additional lifeguard, and you will probably be expected to know the emergency drill and method of artificial respiration your camp uses.

No matter what your special job is, you should know what the camp arrangements and practices are in the following areas:

Swimming

1. The swimming area should be clearly marked off in sections for beginning swimmers, shallow-water swimmers, and deep-water swimmers.

2. The campers may be classified by devices such as coloured caps or tags, making easier the job of identifying each level of swimming ability.

3. There must be adequate and diligent supervision

—no horsing around on the docks or under the water.

4. There should be a definite plan for checking swimmers in and out. Some camps send them in and out of the water in pairs, called "buddies." Know what your camp system is.

5. There will be regular swimming periods, possibly with the camp divided into small groups. Some of these periods are instructional, and some are free swims. Know what is expected of you during each.

6. At times there may be extra dips which require permission from the counselor in charge of swimming. If night dips are permitted the campers will probably wear white bathing-caps and the area must be floodlit, with swimming confined to the inner areas.

7. Much waterfront activity is controlled by a whistle system. Possibly your camp will use one whistle to enter the water and two to come out. Three blasts is almost universally the recognized emergency signal for all swimmers to leave the water immediately.

8. None of your campers should be allowed to swim under boats or docks.

9. You should know where lifebuoys and emergency boat and reaching poles are available. For the most part, the waterfront staff will use these; but who knows—it may be you who is the person on the spot to stretch out a pole to the tiring swimmer.

Boating

Campers become pretty proud, not only of being able to handle a boat skilfully, but of doing so in the approved way —or, as they often call it, "our way." You should learn what the camp ways are regarding loading a canoe; who gets in first, and who gets out last; the accepted method of using a paddle; making landings; lifting the canoe out of the water; and storing canoe and paddle properly.

Of course you know that a canoe or a rowboat filled with water will not sink—that it is capable of supporting several people; that if a boat capsizes, you hang onto it and never leave it in an attempt to swim to shore. Your boating instructor will teach you how to right a capsized canoe, and will provide opportunities for you to learn how to feel more and more at home on the water.

In general, what has been said about canoeing applies also to sailing and to the use of power boats and other small craft. The rules of right of way for water craft are increasingly important and should be known to every person in camp. These will probably be discussed with you at an early staff meeting.

It may be that you have been "brought up on the water" and know all about it. This is good, but it is important that you put yourself out to follow the camp rules while you are employed, and not your own. You may be able to discuss with your director some of the advantages of your own methods, and the camp may decide to incorporate them; if so, you have made a real contribution. Don't get off to a bad start, however, by saying, "This is the way we did it at our cottage," or at some other camp you have attended. Conform first, then reconstruct.

Exploring Around the Camp

Woods are the safest and friendliest places in the world, provided that you are properly dressed to enjoy them and that you don't get lost. Clothing is important. The barefoot boy is picturesque, but not practical. Proper shoes are essential, and if you are really going into the bush, you should wear slacks, not shorts.

Your camp will have boundaries beyond which you and your campers cannot go without obtaining permission. When you do wander afar, know your area or take a map; know how to use a compass and how to follow trails. If you stray from the trail, mark the path you have taken so that you may find your way back. A good explorer can always find his way back. Don't wait until you are lost to use your compass; use it on the way in. Remember, it often takes longer to come back than to go, because you are more tired. A good watch will help you allow time for the return journey.

If you become lost, the best thing to do is sit and wait until you are found. The only thing that can hurt you is panic. Your comrades know you are lost and will set out to search for you. If you wander or run blindly, you make discovery that much more difficult. Find a clearing or move to the open shore; then sit and wait. Shout every fifteen or twenty minutes; or better still, blow a whistle—it penetrates much farther than your voice. Gather firewood in case you have to spend the night in the bush. Take stock of everything you have with you, and see what you can use to make yourself comfortable until you are found.

You may decide to explore the camp road which leads to the highway. Remember, always walk single file, facing traffic. Never let your campers become involved in hitchhiking. Ask your director about liability and traffic hazards; also be sure you know whether he permits counselors to hitchhike.

If you go to camp as part of the advance party probably one of your duties will be to help check the buildings, waterfront, and play areas to see that they are free from accident hazards. You will probably be instructed in some form of fire drill. You may be asked to help put play areas in good condition, especially those in which you will be particularly involved.

You should certainly examine your own cabin, specially for cracked boards, loose railings, unsafe steps, protruding nails, and broken furniture, and report these to the director. See that screens are in good condition and learn where you obtain supplies of fly and mosquito repellent. Note the place where your campers are to keep their flashlights, so they can be reached in the dark. And, of course, you should know

---

PRINCIPLES FOR TEACHING SAFETY

In teaching safety from infancy to adulthood, there are principles which are effective at any level. Adults should provide:

1. a good example by *always* observing safety rules;
2. protection until a child is ready physically, emotionally, and mentally for a given experience;
3. instruction—given casually in the course of everyday living, given specifically when a child is ready for a new experience;
4. practice under supervision, so that faults can be corrected and a good pattern set—there may thus be assurance that safety rules have been not only learned by rote but incorporated into a child's way of living;
5. opportunity to carry on alone when training is considered adequate;
6. continued awareness as to progress or lack of progress in responsibility;
7. a period of retraining, with temporary withdrawal of the privilege of carrying on alone, if safety rules have been disregarded;
8. opportunity to try again to prove that knowledge will be put to use and responsibility accepted.

*Frances Johnson**

---

*From the *Bulletin* of the Institute of Child Study, University of Toronto.

where fire extinguishers are and how they are used; also where buckets of water are kept, and whether you are responsible for seeing that they are kept filled. You should know where there are poison ivy and other noxious weeds, so that you can keep campers away from them.

Day by Day

There are day-by-day things to do about safety. Your cabin and the ground around it are your responsibility. Check frequently, and report that broken step as quickly as possible. Also, in or around camp, if you are the person to see a loose tree limb or a piece of broken glass, do something about it. You have two responsibilities—one is doing, the other is reporting. No matter how well the director has planned, it is only through your vigilance that the camp can be kept safe all the time.

HEALTH

Camp should be an ideal place for developing and promoting physical and mental well-being in children, but it is impossible for any one person—the director, the doctor, or the nurse—to assume the responsibility of seeing that the health needs of every camper will be met. This requires the full co-operation of every counselor.

You, with your contacts with the small cabin group, have two distinct responsibilities. One, you should get to know the state of health of each of your campers and be sensitive to any abnormality. Two, you should carry out any particular health program prescribed by the medical staff for any one of your campers. If the doctor advises extra rest for one of your group, you *must* see that these instructions are adhered to, and organize that camper's day so that he is living within these requirements and yet finding pleasant things to do. If a camper is unable to take part in strenuous activity, do not just leave him alone; plan a quieter activity, such as crafts or sketching. In this way a period of restricted activity can become a happy one for the child. If the doctor forbids Johnny to swim after a cold, you *must* make certain he does not swim, and must also find interesting things for him to do during the swimming period.

Rest and Activity

The success of a camp is not measured by the amount of strenuous activity in progress. Camp is the children's holiday, and it should be a time of leisure and restfulness without either physical over-exertion or mental high tension. Fatigue can be a real problem for your campers.

Children differ greatly in the amount of rest they need and in the extent to which they are affected by excitement. You should try to recognize these differences and adapt the program to meet the needs of individual campers. In health more than any other field, the program should be made for the campers, not the campers for the program. Signs of fatigue are easily recognized in the tired appearance and irritable, emotional behaviour of a child; noisiness and high, shrill voices often indicate over-stimulation rather than good healthy fun.

Within your group you may find a child who simply runs on his nerves. Such a child is usually underweight and easily upset, and wants to do everything all at once. Help him organize and conserve his energy by emphasizing quieter activities, done one at a time. Another child may be in perfectly good condition but simply lazy. He may want to sit around growing fatter each day. In such a case you will try to get him going.

In addition to these individual differences in rest requirements, there are certain times and situations in camp which must be carefully controlled to prevent over-activity and stimulation. The program at the beginning of the camp period must allow for gradual increase of activity. Children have come directly from the city, often from a week or two of school examinations. They are not used to the sunshine and outdoor life, or to the experience of living with a group of people and eating meals in a dining-room where a great many things are going on around them. Food and water changes may cause some eliminative disturbances, excitement may cause nausea; and with some children such upsets may result in homesickness. Activities in the cabin group should be stressed during these days, rather than programs for the camp as a whole. Spending the first few days simply fixing up the cabin and exploring the surroundings, with short swimming periods free from tests or classes, is likely to be encouraged by your camp.

The last week of long-term camps has often been in danger of becoming too exciting. Large events, such as regattas, sports days, and special shows, are nowadays, in most good camps, organized throughout the last two weeks rather than left for the last few days. Some camps which have a closing banquet find it valuable to hold it the second-to-last night of camp, leaving the last day for cabin-group activities of packing and tidying, with a quiet evening program before the long trip home is begun.

With girls you should allow for extra rest during menstrual periods and, although these should in no way be considered illnesses, most girls should not swim or ride or start on strenuous canoe trips, at least during the first few days. There are vast differences in the degree to which girls are affected. You, the cabin counselor, must be the person to recognize their needs. The regularity of periods may be disturbed with the change to camp life. You may have to reassure the camper that this is quite natural. Some girls may have their first period during camp. You may have to advise on sanitary measures, explain the matter, and lessen possible embarrassment. If you do not feel competent to do so, call on the camp nurse or doctor or your section or camp director.

Although individual differences must be allowed for at all times, the following table indicates the minimum amount of sleep needed by the average child:

Age   6 to 12—11 hours
      12 to 15—10 hours
      15 to 18— 9 hours

In addition to this, an afternoon rest hour is essential. It is not necessary for campers to rest in their cabins, which are often warm at noon and offer many opportunities for social play; a rug under a shady tree or a favourite spot in the hills may be used, provided the child really rests. On very warm days you might extend rest hour into the late afternoon by conversation, quiet games, or stories in the shady nooks. By arranging quiet interests, you can provide extra rest pleasantly.

A camp which is firm about making rest hour and lights-out matters of definite requirement has the greatest chance of being a healthy camp. You should see that rest *means* rest, and should remember that you too need sleep and rest if you are to do an efficient job!

Inspection and care

Daily inspection is a most important feature of keeping campers well. For young campers, this inspection should include a complete checkover of skin, inquiries regarding daily elimination or colds, and observation of the general appearance and behaviour of each child. For older campers, use tactful questioning and observation. In this way, by noticing anything unusual and immediately reporting it to the doctor or nurse, you can usually prevent the development of severe illness and the spread of communicable diseases. For example, if you detect and report a camper's cough when it first appears, it may prevent that camper from having to spend a week in the infirmary with bronchitis. Very few campers will complain of a cough, because they know it may mean a few days out of the water. Similarly, by noticing a skin lesion and reporting it, you may prevent impetigo from spreading to cabin-mates or even further.

It is important that you do not ignore or minimize small cuts or symptoms of illness. A little antiseptic and a plastic bandage today are far better than penicillin and hot compresses tomorrow. You must see that these things are looked after promptly; campers are too busy to bother. Do not send a camper to the nurse, take him yourself. If you don't, he may wander out of sight, lean against a tree for a while, then come back and tell you, "The nurse says I'm fine."

Never diagnose and never treat, even with a plastic bandage. The medical staff is there because of its highly specialized skill and knowledge. Use it. If the doctor or nurse tells you to bring a camper back at a certain time or to see that something is done, follow the instructions carefully.

If the camper is confined to the medical centre, find out the visiting hours and don't miss opportunities to visit. That camper needs you. Try to bring a book, game, flower, anything of interest that will brighten his day. Most important of all is your cheerful presence. Perhaps his cabin-mates could make a get-well card or write a group letter. They may even be permitted to talk through a screen window from a distance, if this will not disturb other patients. Once the camper is permitted to return to the group, you must see that there is a balance between rest and exercise for a few days. Follow the nurse's instructions. Campers will usually be too ambitious and want to overdo it.

Communicable Diseases

Although every child comes to camp with a medical certificate stating that he has not had any known contact with measles, chicken pox, whooping cough, etc., these diseases do appear in camps. During the first day at camp, possibly before the doctor or nurse has examined every child, it is particularly important that counselors report any signs of illness, as it is then that communicable diseases are most likely to appear.

Sore throat, headache, general malaise, gastrointestinal disturbances, cough, fever, and later skin rash, are all danger signals, which may be symptoms of an infectious disease and hence should be reported by you to the doctor without delay. It is not necessary for counselors to be alarmists, but the importance of alert observation cannot be over-emphasized.

First Aid and Emergencies

You should be familiar with the fundamentals of first aid. This is particularly necessary if you are taking campers on canoe and riding trips, or on long hikes, or for camp craft, as these are activities in which accidents are most likely to occur. It is absolutely essential for you to know the first-aid treatment for burns, cuts, fractures, dislocations, sprains, and bites, and the application of artificial respiration. The details of first-aid treatment are readily available in excellent handbooks and most camps provide first-aid courses for their counselors.

All accidents and injuries which occur in or close to camp, regardless of their apparent insignificance, must be reported to the camp doctor or nurse. On trips some distance away from camp, injuries should be dealt with according to first-aid principles; and if they are serious, medical help should be sought as soon as possible. You should realize that the camp doctor and director are responsible if a serious complication arises from an injury which has been treated improperly or not referred to a doctor as soon as possible. Hence when you are confronted with an accident, limit your treatment to first aid and get medical help without delay.

On trips out of camp, it is essential that you restrain campers from drinking water from wells, streams, or lakes. One cannot depend upon the clear, clean appearance of water, and it is always safer to use water which has been purified by boiling or by chemical treatment. Be sure you know how to use chlorine tablets or chlorination kits—how much chlorine for how much water, and how long to let it stand before use.

On camping trips, there is one illness which demands special attention, namely, acute appendicitis. It may occur rarely during camp, but when it does, it is serious, and in children, a real emergency. The commonest manifestations are persistent abdominal pain, nausea and vomiting, accompanied by fever and, later, abdominal tenderness. Needless to say, every conceivable variation of these symptoms is possible, but if you are suspicious of appendicitis, there is only *one thing to do*—take the child to the doctor; and *one thing not to do*—never give the child a laxative on the assumption that he has a stomach ache. This is because of the simple mechanical danger of rupturing the appendix.

Food

The average dietary requirements are present in regular camp meals, as planned by an efficient dietitian. When extra nourishment is required for certain campers, it will be supervised by the doctor or nurse. Campers should be expected to eat what is set before them, and wide deviation from the common diet over any period of time should not be allowed. Report such cases to the camp nurse.

Every girls' camp has its quota of reducers. In most instances dieting should be discouraged. It is best dealt with by substituting a genuine interest in the study of dietetics and food values under the guidance of the camp dietitian. You can do a great deal by your own example. Consult the doctor or nurse about campers who insist on dieting.

Some campers have genuine allergies to particular foods; you should know about these. Don't force a child to eat fish if the child tells you he mustn't; but if you doubt his word, check with the doctor. On the other hand, with all the prevailing food fads children hear about, don't be concerned with the camper who says, "I never can eat beets, and neither can Father," or, "Onions simply don't agree with me." Never force food, and fuss as little as possible about it; expect the child to eat, and he probably will.

A word about pills and medicines, Many campers bring a variety of these from home. They are not averse to sharing them with their friends. All such medicines should be turned in to the nurse or doctor, who will keep them or will instruct you on their use. These are not samples to be given away. What is essential to one child may be poison to another. See that the right child gets his prescribed medication at the right time in a matter-of-fact way. Beyond that, the less talk and discussion about medication the better.

Simple Health Measures

Ordinary body cleanliness and dental care frequently need your tactful prompting, and direct supervision may be essential. With young children particularly, it is necessary to see that sufficient and appropriate clothing is worn on cold or rainy days.

If an evening dip is allowed, counselors should be certain that the children's hair and ears are dry before they go to bed.

Head covering should be obligatory when the campers are exposed to the sun for any length of time, and sun glasses should be worn by those sensitive to strong light.

Sunburn is unnecessary and foolish in most cases. Exposure to the sun should be gradual, a few minutes a day at first. Be particularly alert on canoe trips or any time you are on the water. The attitude that only careless campers and counselors get bad sunburns can be developed in camp, and will help to avoid the painful and sometimes serious results of a burn.

Your camp will teach you to identify the poisonous plants

of your area, and what to do if a camper contacts them. If there are poisonous snakes, be sure you know how to use a snake-bite kit. Never let campers eat unknown berries even though they look good, and mushrooms should be left untouched, even by hand, unless you are sure of their identity.

Special orders for the health care of any campers, covering medicine, diet, or routine, should be given in writing by the physician to the counselor concerned, and it is imperative that each detail be carried out to the letter.

A healthy summer is a happy summer. Health is the basic requirement of every parent for his child. To maintain it requires your continual vigilance.

Chapter Five

YOU WILL GROW TOO

Elizabeth Raymer

Now let us think about *you*. From these first chapters you will have gained a number of ideas about your group of campers and about understanding and guiding them as they grow towards maturity. Behind this advice has been the implication that you will be growing too and that you will be trying to develop those qualities which are important for leadership. A counselor's job at camp is like the familiar illustration of a pebble thrown into a still pond. It makes ripples. This is the way your personality will make itself felt in the group. Do not feel insulted because you are not likened to a great rock making an enormous splash. Great splashes make navigation difficult.

The circle nearest to you, your first area of responsibility, is the *campers*. The camp is for the campers and you are there to see that they are guided, taught, cared for, loved and understood; they are your first and greatest concern.

Next come the *activities,* the things you do with the campers. These are many and varied. Some of them will depend only upon you; others will fit into the camp's carefully worked-out program. You will be expected to discharge these responsibilities ably and enthusiastically.

The third area of your duties lies in the field of *counselor-counselor relations*. You will be working with other people, perhaps with quite a large staff; and how you do your job can affect every member of that staff. That is how important you are!

Let us consider some of the qualities which are important in a good camp counselor. You will have all of these already to some degree, but in none will you be perfect. No one is. You might well assess the extent to which you already have them, and during camp check yourself on your progress in increasing them.

It may astonish you to learn that the most frequently named cause for failure in any job is, "He can't get along with other people." *Good relationships with others* are as important in counseling as in most jobs. You realize that nearly everyone can increase this social skill, so make use of all the opportunities you can for practising it.

Try to increase your ability to put self-interest aside and devote your efforts to others. This does not mean abject self-abasement or the martyrdom of denying yourself pleasure. It is simply the difference between getting and giving. It is the transfer from being a camper to being a counselor; it is the growth from student to teacher—indeed, from child to adult. It is the difference between practising a dive and teaching a child the skill, forgetting all about your own practice. It is even more than that; ultimately it is the state of getting more satisfaction from seeing the child learn the dive than from learning it yourself. This comes fairly easy to some counselors; to others it is a task requiring conscious and conscientious effort. By going through the motions of the skill, the skill may become yours. It is a joyous and happy kind of skill, full of rewards; you will use it all your life. Increase in it is real progress toward maturity.

The extent to which you have matured is shown by your ability to control your emotions and to behave as a sensible, intelligent adult. Losing one's temper, feeling hurt, entertaining unreasonable fears, giving way to fits of depression, sprinkling every conversation with "I," indecisiveness, resenting criticism, jealousy, and constant striving for popularity are indications of immaturity. There are, as you know from experience and observation, many more examples.

The mature person searches for the reasons behind his own behaviour and that of others. He acknowledges the necessity for rules and regulations, he does not descend to a childish level in dealing with a child's unreasonable behaviour. He looks ahead to the consequences of his actions and those of the group he is leading. He doesn't grumble about things he can do nothing about, such as rainy weather and no wind for sailing. He surveys a situation from a positive viewpoint and does what can be done under the circumstances. So if you are growing towards maturity you will strive to control your less desirable forms of juvenile behaviour.

As a camp counselor, you are expected to act as an adult; and you will not find this role too difficult to play, because there is help all around you. Among your staff associates you will find enviable examples of this maturity. When you are in doubt say to yourself, "What would so-and-so do in such a case?" and pattern your behaviour accordingly. This is a very useful technique. Nor are you so old that you cannot remember some outstanding and seemingly perfect leader of your childhood. Think of that leader's qualities. Try them out yourself. It will assist you toward self-possession, self-control, self-confidence, and good judgment.

Good judgment is another quality of the mature person. It is primarily a matter of thinking ahead. It is being able to answer the question, "What do I do now and what will happen then?" Every waking hour you will be called upon to exercise your judgment. Children are not static little vegetables sitting in a row; they are constantly busy. It will require the use of all your senses to be aware of what is going on.

Hearing a group of eight boys planning to get their hunting knives out of their trunks should mean to you a situation which demands your immediate attention. Survey the present stage of the activity, casually inquire its purpose, assess the feeling of the group—belligerence, or innocent purposefulness—and estimate your own ability to supervise eight sharp knives in untrained hands. You will have to do all this in a very few seconds, and arrive at a solution of the problem—perhaps a proposal that the boys take turns working on the project, or a suggestion that it be abandoned temporarily for something more fascinating.

You will have to decide whether or not a proposed project is too far, too windy, too deep, too difficult, too rowdy, too quiet, and so on. Your decisions will encompass clothing, weather, activities, other people, whose job it is, food and eating habits, stories and reading material—and whether or not you are the one who should make the decision. Your decision may sometimes have to be an unpopular one; and you will not be right every time—none of us is. The important thing is that you do not make the same mistake over again.

Mistakes are not bad in themselves; it is what you do about them that really counts. Just about the most damning excuse a counselor can offer is, "I didn't think." You *must* think; think a long way ahead, and govern yourself accordingly. The necessity for good judgment in working with children cannot be overstated. But lest you become pompous and pedantic, never put aside your sense of humour.

The wise use of your *sense of humour* develops with increased maturity. If the situation is ridiculous, laugh! Laughter clears the air; laughter unifies a group. Laughter, which distinguishes human beings from animals, promotes a feeling of well-being and good mental and physical buoyancy. A sense of humour and the ability to laugh will make it much easier for you to get along with children. They are full of humour. One of the things you will have to remember and which you will undoubtedly have to teach children is that the secret is laughing *with* and not *at*. At yourself, yes; at children, never. Unless of course it is a comedy performance and you are the audience! Often laughter is inaudible, it resides in the twinkle of your eye or hovers around your mouth; but it is there. With it you are approachable and invite confidence. Without it you lose' your sense of values and may appear to be intolerant of another's shortcomings and idiosyncrasies.

Tolerance is that live-and-let-live attitude which tempers your prejudices and broadens your outlook. There are always at least two points from which to view every problem or circumstance. You may feel that you are very broad-minded; most young people do feel this. But check! How many strong dislikes, hates and aversions do you have? How do you express your opinion—as a statement of fact, or merely as a belief?

Children are very sensitive to adult attitudes; and they too deserve to be heard and to have their viewpoints carefully considered. Remember yourself at that age. You slipped and faltered now and then, your knowledge of life was incomplete and your judgment faulty; but you were learning, and you learned best and most from adults who would listen to you with an open mind.

You must be tolerant of youthful nonsense and shortcomings, and endlessly patient in teaching. It is the unusual person who learns anything the first time it is presented. Making a bed, building a fire, clearing a table, or paddling a canoe requires repetitive instruction and practice under the guidance of a counselor who is tolerant of mistakes, and who recognizes each sign of progress with encouragement and praise. The most inviting lake on a warm and sparkling day may appear large and dark and forbidding to the non-swimmer. The activities of the proficient swimmers may appear impossibly complicated to him. He may be fearful. He will not learn to swim in one lesson, or in two. Cast your mind back again to childhood. Can you hear the echoing words, "Please close the door quietly," said over and over again, with patience and tolerance? Remember that quiet admonitions, constructively and politely given, were most acceptable to you.

Courtesy, consideration and good manners have a function to perform in smoothing the rough spots of daily living in a group. You would rather be called by your own name than as "you in the plaid shirt." So would everyone else. Thoughtfulness of the comfort of others, children and adults, has just as much place in the great outdoors as at an important city function. The use of "please" and "thank you" are more than just habits of speech. They mark the speaker as one who respects his fellow human beings. One of the ways that children learn is by imitating the people they admire and respect. Provide a good example and reap the rewards of being treated politely.

Wholesomeness is one of the most important characteristics of a counselor. The fact that a camp provides a community which temporarily isolates its members from the rest of the world gives camping an opportunity denied to almost all other aspects of youth work. At camp children can take part in worth-while activities in a healthful environment, and you as a counselor are an important part of that environment. You should create an atmosphere of high ideals—not goody-goody, but good. Attitudes toward work and play, ethical living, their own religious faith, and their own adulthood are being shaped by these campers. Everything you do and say should be making a worthy and positive contribution to this environment. This may at first require a certain amount of self-discipline on your part, but self-discipline is something you will need throughout life.

A counselor must be able to show campers how to do all sorts of things. Depending upon the size and the organization of the camp, you will need to be able to do a creditable job of teaching one or two outdoor skills. It is not enough that you are able to perform the skill well; you will need to know step-by-step methods of presentation. Many camping skills can be learned by performing them after you have become a counselor. This is one of the wonderful advantages; one can keep on acquiring outdoor knowledge forever. But you must have some sort of secure foundation to start with. Children want to learn, they wish to improve their skills; they are not contented with being turned loose to amuse themselves with equipment. Know the answers to "How do you do it?" and "Is this the way?" How do you find out? Take courses, read books, consult the experts. And never be satisfied that you have found the perfect method. Good teachers constantly criticize their own work. Camping provides a nearly perfect teaching situation.

At the first sign that the counselor's interest, enthusiasm and energy are at a low ebb, the camper is lost. *Energy* is essential in dealing with young people. Energy results from rest, good health, and a feeling of general well-being. No group welcomes a tired, despondent, or irritable counselor. Children regard the lazy staff member as a nonentity. You must be able to get up (on time!) in the morning with enthusiasm for the day ahead and with enough energy to carry you through it, with natural tiredness at the end but without chronic fatigue. The campers will be ready for the day's adventures and confidently expect you to join them. Fellow staff members will expect you to perform all of your camp duties without fail, and with a cheerful competence.

Naturally, if your *health* is precarious, camp is not for you; but you may, in spite of your usual good health, become ill during the camping period. As an adult, you will be expected to accept your affliction without grumbling, follow the doctor's instructions implicitly, stay in bed until you are told you may get up, and then go back to work without abject feelings of guilt, and without complaint. In day-to-day living you should be mature enough to eat sensibly, sleep well, and apply the rules of good health you are supposed to be teaching the children. With good health and with normal energy, you will be able to face all the aspects of your job.

Camp life demands *adaptability* from everyone—campers, counselors, directors, cooks, handymen. This is one of the good qualities that life in the outdoors helps you acquire. Sunshine, rain, wind, heat, and storm require us to adjust to them. The weather teaches us to accept the inevitable and to use our ingenuity in remaining comfortable and happy. Ask yourself how you can increase your adaptability to other things, such as routine and unexpected changes from routine. You may have to adapt your concept of your job so that it will fit without conflict into the total picture of the camp. You will certainly have to be able to adapt yourself to living with other people.

Inflexible people create very awkward situations. But those who have the vision and the common sense to take the whole situation into consideration usually have no difficulty in seeing the necessity of adapting themselves to changing circumstances. If you regard routine as irritating, it will be an irritation which grows more severe each day. But if you regard it as a necessity when a number of people are living together, it can become a source of freedom. All the ordinary details of the day—when and what to eat, when to get up in the morning—have been decided. The time and effort you would require for making such decisions, you can use for more constructive purposes.

Your influence is not limited to camp life; it is felt even in the homes of the children. You write letters to parents, and meet and talk with them when they visit. Your sayings and doings will be described throughout the months ahead. The evidence of your care for each child will go with him when he returns home.

What will *you* get out of it all? Your greatest gains from a summer of counseling will be from the intangibles. The truth that the more you put into it, the more you get out of it is strikingly apparent in camping. You learn how to do things, thus increasing your knowledge and self-assurance; you experience the joys and the irritations of living and working with people and learning much about human nature.

Are you formulating your own philosophy of education, camping, and life? Are you becoming better able to test your own ideas? Are you learning to profit from constructive criticism? Are you experiencing the inexpressible, joyous satisfaction of teaching children and seeing them learn—and the warmth of affection that children are eager to give to respected leaders? Is your awareness of the universe through the expansion of your senses growing? Are you garnering new physical and spiritual resources? Are you making friends and enjoying your work with them? Are you having fun, lots of fun?

If so, you, as well as your campers, are growing towards maturity.

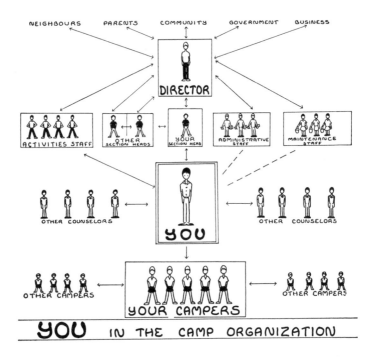

YOU IN THE CAMP ORGANIZATION

Drawn by Marjorie Wilson

Whatever camp you attend, you will be related to several groups of people: your campers, counselors who are your equals on the staff, supervisors to whom you are responsible, the teaching, administrative, and maintenance staffs—and, of course, the director. The director is responsible for everything that happens in the camp, and through him you are related to parents, tradesmen, community and government.

In a small camp some of the staff will hold more than one position. In a large camp several people may have similar positions. But all these positions must be filled for a camp to operate, and you will be related to all the people involved and the jobs they do. Remember it is the director who is responsible for every decision made and action taken by any member of the staff, including *you*. These may affect the camp's public relations, legal matters, camp business, the neighbours and community, and above all *the welfare of a child*.

PART II

Your Part In the Camp Program

Chapter Six

A COUNSELOR'S TYPICAL DAY

Barry G. Lowes

To me, the ideal summer is that of a cabin counselor. The friends you make, the memories you store up, the rich dividends in human relations that you gain, will enrich all the rest of your life. It is not a coincidence that so many of our outstanding men and women of today were camp counselors yesterday. I must warn you that there is a magic about camping. It gets into your blood and you cannot get it out. It will stay with you for life.

The greatest single factor that will determine the happiness and success of a camper's summer is you, the counselor. You are responsible twenty-four hours a day for everything that happens to your campers. Their behaviour will be governed by your example more than by anything else. You will be judged by your actions, not by your words.

Not everything said here will apply directly to your particular camp, and some of it will seem like old stuff to you. I will try to point out some of the important little extra things that make the difference between an excellent counselor and one who just does an adequate job. No matter how different our camps may be, we have one thing in common: we all work with children. These children all have the same basic needs. Therefore, the basic things discussed here can readily be adapted to your own particular camp and your own group.

STARTING THE DAY

Set a good example from the first day. Be the first one up. Once your eyes are open, check the weather and dress accordingly. Too often you see counselors coming to breakfast in jackets, gloves and scarves, while their campers come in T-shirts. Long pants and jackets to breakfast are safe bets on any day. It may be wise to wear rubber boots, for a heavy dew can soak shoes more than a rain.

Check your campers for symptoms of illness. If your suspicions are aroused, be sure to take them to the nurse for the morning clinic. Make washing, brushing of teeth, and hair combing a set routine, and see that it is carried out. Morning dips under supervision can be fun for some. You had better check with your camp director as to the policy about this. Washing in the river or lake can be a beautiful tradition for a cabin group. Go slowly and quietly, pausing for a moment at the water's edge to listen and watch.

When you start for breakfast, don't leave any stragglers behind. If the campers tend to pair off, walk with the loner, the one who is left out. With younger children, one counselor should stay behind and pull back the covers on each bed. From time to time you will find a wet bed. If so, strip it immediately and take the wet linen to the laundry. Re-make the bed. There is no need for the occurrence to be public knowledge. Treat bed wetting matter-of-factly, as an accident that could happen to anyone. Beware of teasing and ridicule by other campers. If the accident occurs frequently, discuss it with the camp doctor or nurse.

STANDARDS AT MEALS

It is vitally important that all campers wash their hands after toileting and before all meals. Check them; don't assume that they have all washed.

While the method of food service varies from camp to

camp, certain general responsibilities will be the same. Always serve the campers first. A counselor never heaps up his plate and then passes the remainder along to the campers. Serving the children guarantees a fair share, plus variety, for everyone. Left to their own choice, most of them will eat meat and potatoes but few vegetables.

The manners of your campers will be determined by the tone that you set during the first few days of camp. Set your expectations high. As with all behaviour, you will generally get what they think you expect of them. They will test you in manners as in all discipline. Don't nag; be firm but pleasant. At the outset, squelch grabbing, yelling, using hands, mixing all their food into one pile of mush, or deliberately spilling things to gain attention. Some campers will bolt their food as though they feared losing it to someone else. They may have sound reasons from experiences at home to justify their behaviour. Make it clear that there will be enough for everyone, and that no seconds will be served until everyone has finished his first helping.

Discourage the campers who make a face or say "Ugh!" when certain food comes on the table. As a counselor, you should never criticize the food by word, expression, or gesture. If you feel that something is wrong, tell the director later. He is the only one who can set the situation right.

Never chastise a camper in front of the others, or cause him to lose face. Sit the worst offender beside you, where you can control him without disturbing the other campers. Never, never, never withhold food. Desserts are the favourite thumbscrew of poor counselors. Food is not a privilege, it is a right. If a camper is misbehaving badly, perhaps you should have him sit quietly and eat after the others have left. If you ever feel that it is necessary to withhold food, discuss it with the director first.

Don't force anyone to eat. Campers should be encouraged to try a little of everything, but never forced. Often a well-meaning counselor will load up a small child's plate. This can overwhelm a child. It is better to serve smaller portions and have the camper ask for seconds. I can find no justification for withholding a camper's dessert because he does not finish all of the main course. A meal consists of several courses and he is entitled to all of them. On the other hand, he should not be allowed to fill up on extra desserts. If you feel that a camper is not eating enough, or not eating the right things, consult the nurse. Children never deliberately starve themselves to death, although parents and young counselors have been known to worry themselves almost to death.

If you have a new or shy camper, sit him beside you. The first few meals can be overwhelming for a newcomer. If you sit him at the far end of the table, he may starve.

Do not permit campers to take any food from the dining-hall for either a sick camper or a tired counselor. If there are any extra desserts, they must be shared equally and fairly, not kept for the counselors alone. See that your campers salt their food, for they lose a great deal of salt through sweating.

Mealtime should be a time for fun and conversation that is interesting, light, and on a high plane. However, when someone asks for quiet, keep your group quiet. So often I see counselors at a table with their hands raised for quiet, but their tongues going a mile a minute.

Cleaning Up the Cabin

Clean-up can be either a drudgery or a simple necessity, depending upon you. Again, your attitude is all-important. I suggest that you adopt the attitude, "Let's do it fast and well and get it over with." Try to establish pride in your cabin. If you play the role of Simon Legree, the children will outlast you, I promise. Make a duty chart or wheel that has each person's name on it and the duties for each day of the week.

Be sure that you add *your* name to it. It is a good idea to have one camper as supervisor each day. This spreads the role of "dirty guy" around. Besides, campers get a big kick out of being able to inspect your bed and shelves.

Clean-up can afford young campers an ideal opportunity to help one another. You should move about helping them, joking, talking, making it fun. Sweeping is difficult for young campers. You may have to go back over it later. Beware of the youngsters who strip their beds, throw the sheets, pillow and blankets on the floor, and then walk all over them while they make their beds. It happens.

You must inspect campers' shelves regularly. Without thinking, they will stuff wet shorts, bathing-suits, or other clothing into the back of their shelves or the bottom of their trunks or laundry bags. If this happens, within a few days you will have a wonderful crop of mildew that can ruin clothing. You must also be on guard against the camper who has an accident in his pants and hides them in his laundry bag.

Once a week—laundry day is often the best day—have a super clean-up; strip your beds, shake out and air your blankets. Take everything off your shelves and out of your trunks. You will be amazed at what you will find.

Cleanliness and Clothing

The most honourable campers will slip up when it comes to cleanliness. They are just too busy. Don't assume that because you tell them to go and wash, it will be done; this is wishful thinking. Make going to the toilet, washing, and brushing their teeth a routine. When the whole cabin group gathers at the lake or around the wash-stand, it can become a lot of fun. Unobtrusively check them and make light of sending someone back to dig out that extra dirt. Joke along with them. A clean counselor with good health habits begets clean campers. The familiar cry heard from campers is, "We swim every day, who needs to wash?" A hot soap bath—that is, a shower, or even a sponge-bath with water heated over an open fire—should be taken at least three times a week; and this should include washing the hair.

You must see that your campers change their clothes regularly. This means girls too, for they can be just as lazy as boys when it comes to cleanliness. Underwear and socks should be changed daily. If your campers have enough clothing, it is a good idea to have them put everything into their laundry bags when they undress at night and put on clean clothes in the morning. Discourage the borrowing and lending of clothing, particularly bathing-suits. Counselors should never borrow from campers, whether it is clothing, flashlights, or anything else.

Check to see that campers do not wear damp bathing-suits or clothing all day. When left on, they can produce a rash or a chill. As wonderful as the sun is, it can be a crippler if campers are over-exposed. See that they wear sun hats, especially when they are out in boats. Gradually increase their exposure to the sun, rather than have them suffer from sunburn. Insects are a part of camp life. Tender campers should be protected from mosquitoes in the early evening and on muggy days, by pulling their socks over their long pants and by wearing long-sleeved shirts that are done up at the wrists and neck.

YOUR PART IN THE PROGRAM

The program is everything that happens during any twenty-four hours, not just at activity periods. If you are sensitive and imaginative, you will see activity possibilities that others miss. Camping is exciting; by its very nature it is filled with adventure—hiking, exploring, rafting, swimming, and sleeping out; but adventurous does not mean dangerous. Safety must be uppermost in your mind at all times. There are two extremes that should be avoided. One is the cotton-wool world that is over-protective; the other is the flagrantly dangerous that courts injury. We have a saying at camp, "If in doubt, don't do it." You must learn to anticipate such hazards as glass, nails, metal, and broken equipment, and thereby avoid them. These should be removed, repaired, or reported. Knives are for campcraft, not for throwing. If campers use them unwisely, they may have to lose the privilege of using them. Painful accidents can be avoided by always using a flashlight at night. Safety should be taught as an integral part of any activity. Teach basic first-aid to your campers. They are interested and learn readily.

Most youngsters like to rough-house, but this should never be done inside the cabin, because it invariably ends in someone's getting hurt. Take the group out on the beach instead and have a good tumble to let off that extra steam. In safety, as in all else, your example is most important.

During the first few days at camp, try to devise projects that will draw your cabin group together, such as a hike, a cook-out, or some other shared adventure. Make up a cabin name, song, and yell. Your camp will have its own particular method of programing. I would like to mention briefly a few important extras.

Too often when choosing activities, democracy is considered to be majority rule. This is a common fallacy. True democracy is not just a matter of the majority outvoting the minority; it includes protecting the rights of the minority, too.

When going to an activity, be on time. If you are late, it shortens the period and spoils the lesson. Help with the instruction if you can, or at least help the instructor to control the group. Remember that you should know your campers best. Join in the activities with them; let your hair down. Activities take on new zest for campers when you participate with them. Besides, you enjoy yourself also. Plan to be with your campers at times other than your scheduled periods, particularly at those free times before meals.

At the end of any activity period, you should ask yourself these questions: Was it fun? What did they learn? How could the activity have been improved? Where will it lead us, or is it a dead-end activity? What happened of significance to the campers?

GENERAL SWIM

Not every camper will want to go to every general swim. However, if absence becomes habitual, try to find the real reason. If for some good reason a camper does not want to go to general swim, encourage him to pursue some other interest—certainly not lying on his bed with a comic book.

Know where your campers are at all times. They should be permitted to wander by themselves or in pairs within a defined area at times, but you should know generally where they are going to be. If you are not on lifeguard duty, take advantage of the opportunity to swim with your group. They will love it. Play games in the shallow area. Buddy-up with the loner, or play with the non-swimmer in the first area. When the swim is over, be sure that your campers dry well, especially their heads, and that they put on shoes and hurry back to the cabin to get out of clammy bathing-suits. The period after general swim is a vulnerable time. When the group gets back to the cabin, if it is unsupervised, the under-dog will be picked on, there will be towel-flicking, water fights, teasing, raiding, and fist fights. These undesirable activities are most common at this time. Therefore, it is vitally important to be with your group.

If activities have been too intensive, over-fatigue can be a big problem. Allow time for relaxation and for leisurely occupations that provide a change of pace.

REST HOUR

Rest hour does not mean swinging from the rafters, trampolining on beds, or running errands. Rest hour *means* rest. The campers need it; this is the time to recharge their batteries. Rest hour fulfils its purpose best when there is a counselor in the cabin. Take advantage of the opportunity to rest yourself. Don't insist on absolute silence, only consideration for others. Some may nap, others may write letters, read, play quiet games, or tell stories. Perhaps on a hot day the group could sit or lie outside in the shade. Lying on his back, a straw between his teeth, gazing up through the pine trees at the white clouds scudding, can be a wonderful experience for any camper. Perhaps a guitar and some soft singing have their place. Rest hour need not be a prison; with imagination it can be transformed into a memorable time.

LETTER WRITING

Your camp will probably have a policy concerning regular letter-writing days. "What shall I say?" you will be asked repeatedly. Help them to tell of their camp accomplishments, things they have done, friends made, and new experiences. While censorship of campers' mail is to be deplored, their writing can certainly be helped and guided. If you were a parent, what would you want to know? And when the letters are ready to be mailed, be sure that the addresses are clearly written.

If one of your campers does not receive mail for several days, discuss the matter with the director. If the situation is serious enough, it might even warrant your writing him a card from town on your day off.

RAINY DAYS

Of one thing you can be certain—at some times during the summer, it is going to rain. Whether these days will be a boon will depend on how well prepared you are. Loneliness can creep in, or teasing, arguing, and fighting can result from being too closely confined for hours. As with everything else in camp, your attitude and example are all-important; they set the tone. So be cheerful and bright and dress colourfully. If you ever feel the need to coast, do it on a sunny day. Rainy days require your reserves of patience, cheerfulness, energy, and resourcefulness. Treat them as opportunities for a change of pace—have ideas and games up your sleeve that are used only on rainy days. (See Chapter VII.)

It never rains out of a blue sky. Be alert to warnings of a change in the weather, such as darkening skies, changing winds, or a ring around the moon, and take steps that will save you problems once rain comes. Make sure that your tent flaps or cabin shutters are fastened down. Slacken the tent ropes slightly. Clear all clothes from your clothesline; they can be hung out again after the rain. Take in sleeping-bags or blankets that are airing. Make sure your firewood is well covered. Finally, check the grounds around your cabin for anything the rain could hurt.

During the rain your first responsibility is to see that your campers are dressed properly in raincoats, hats and boots. If it is cold, add a jacket or sweater also. Each year more and more wise counselors are taking umbrellas to camp. At first the campers may scoff at you, but in a rain there are always some who sidle up to you and say, "Can I get under too?"

HAPPY ENDING

I will not discuss activities for evening programs—this is another large topic in itself. At all evening programs, it is important that you sit with your group, not with other counselors at the back. Keep your group under control and attentive if others are running the program. Participate with them if this is called for. Towards the end of the evening taper off the excitement. Try to end on a quieter mood. Don't let campers get over-tired or over-stimulated just before bedtime. End the day with taps or some other suitable ritual. It can be very beautiful and memorable for your campers. Leave the evening program in ample time to allow for snacks and preparation for bed without rushing and nagging.

Bedtime is the most important forty-five minutes of the day. Don't be what I call a "pull-chain" counselor—that is, one who hurries his campers into bed, pulls the light out, and disappears. Don't short-change your campers during this period, when they are more impressionable than at any other time of day.

Our cabin always had a small fire laid, covered with a ground sheet, and a small supply of firewood to one side, also covered. We didn't use it every evening but it was always ready when the time seemed opportune. There is something warm, intimate and magnetic about a small fire shared by a cabin group. We used to sit around it, reviewing the day and planning for tomorrow. Sometimes we would have a quiet song, or a snack; but often a snack can destroy the mood that you are trying to create. At the end of this ten or fifteen minutes we used to stand and put our arms around the shoulders of the persons next to us and all look into the fire for a few moments of silence and meditation. We ended with a prayer that was our own cabin prayer. No one spoke or broke the silence until we were back inside the cabin.

Go to the wash-house as a group. When you get back, count heads—make a routine of this. Do not make the common mistake of having children brush their teeth and get into bed, and then giving them candy or a snack.

Check your boys; many of them will want to wear their underwear under their pajamas. This is not a healthy practice. Check the warmth of your campers. On cold nights, I would suggest that they put on a pair of clean socks and a sweatshirt or a sweater. By folding the lower blanket in two and putting the top one singly over it to bind it in, you can create three thicknesses from two blankets. Discourage the nightly use of a sleeping-bag for camp periods longer than ten to fourteen days. Most sleeping-bags do not have a removable lining, so they become dirty and unhealthy from prolonged use. If a sleeping-bag is used, it should be aired often in direct sunlight. Campers should not be permitted to sleep together. It is too crowded, and it is also a psychologically vulnerable situation.

Prayers should be a natural part of going to bed. Unfortunately, many teen-age counselors are going through a self-conscious period about prayers. This is unfortunate because, as in everything else, your attitude and practice will set the tone. It is best if you kneel and pray with them. If you cannot, then set aside a quiet period with the lights out during which each can pray in his own way. If some do not wish to, then they should just lie quietly and respect the rights of others.

Once the lights are out, take five minutes to go quietly from bed to bed. Sitting on the edge of their beds, speak to each camper briefly, quietly, confidentially and reassuringly. Talk about some event of particular significance to him that occurred during the day. Congratulate him on some deed or gesture that he might feel went unnoticed. If he was upset by something during the day, clarify it and reassure him. Leave a camper feeling secure, wanted, and warm inside, by always ending on a pleasant note. Put their worlds together for them. This can be a lonely time of day for some. Five minutes spent wisely each night like this will pay greater dividends than anything else that you do as a counselor. Don't miss the opportunity. I have used this successfully with every age group from six to sixteen.

Spiritual Values

I did not discuss spiritual values under any particular part of the day, because they are learned all day, all week, any time, not just at services. Each day there are innumerable opportunities to teach them; and the sensitive, alert counselor will catch such moments.

God seems to be closer at camp. Sometimes He seems hard to find in our cities, with the hectic pace, the complexities, the pressures, the gaudiness. Camp is stripped of these trappings. Our opportunities for imparting spiritual values are, therefore, all the greater.

Chapter Seven

PROGRAM IDEAS

Joyce Bertram & Barry G. Lowes

CABIN AND CAMP ACTIVITIES

If you want to succeed as a camp counselor, you should be a walking sponge for all the ideas you have seen in practice, heard of, or read about. Although at many camps you will find that there is a program director who is in charge of the program ("everything that happens to a child from the time he gets off the bus"), volunteers with new ideas are always welcomed with open arms. Besides, a counselor's job is twenty-four hours a day; and few, if any, program directors plan for all twenty-four! As a result, you will find yourself with plenty of opportunities to take a hand in program.

You should know your own campers and their abilities and talents better than anyone else does. If you have a youngster who can play the recorder, mouth-organ, or banjo, try to persuade him or her to perform at the camp-fire or musical evening. A child who is confident of your backing in a thing like this is more willing to make a contribution to the group. In this same connection, many children will reveal unexpected ability when you take part in the program yourself—when you are willing to dress up as the old woman who lived in a shoe, or as Father in *Cheaper by the Dozen.*

You are often, also, in the best position to relay program ideas from campers to the program director or the camper council. Where a child will think twice before telling the program director that she is sick to death of canoeing and sailing and wants nothing so much as a morning spent catching minnows or hiking up the nearest mountain, you can pick up this type of information simply by being around with your eyes and ears open and your mouth closed. Awareness of the climate of the group when programs are being planned can save everyone a good many headaches and misunderstandings.

Participation is the great concern of educators and recreation people all over the world. With TV, professional sports, movies, and pre-digested craft kits, children and adults have become increasingly prone to the disease of "spectatoritis." Children will watch puppets on TV with no thought of making their own; they will watch a children's party or a square dance, without the thought occurring to them that they could be doing it themselves. This is where you can help. You wouldn't be camping at all unless you had discovered for yourself the wonderful pleasure which comes from actually *doing* things. Why watch someone on TV bake a cake? Let's get out the reflector oven and bake our own! Why watch a country hoedown? Get out and square-dance yourself! Many youngsters who come to camp have not had the experience of doing many things first-hand. *Camp is the place for participation, not perfection.* Encourage all your campers to *try*; no one cares if the result is not perfect. But the initiative often has to come from you.

Unfortunately, all children do not have the background of experience to allow them to choose what they want to do. Perhaps they are not sure just what the possibilities of the program are. Here is where it is important that you have ideas. Start early to compile a list of games, stunts, skits, and ideas for all occasions. Experienced counselors keep a winter notebook for jotting down camp ideas as they flash fleetingly across the mind. Don't expect to remember them months later unless you write them down.

One of your big responsibilities at many camps will be providing a program for Cabin Night, Bunk Night, or whatever it may be called. At this time you and your charges are on your own for the evening (or it may be a morning or afternoon). All right now, what will you do?

Depending upon the time at your disposal, there are many things you can do. Take them all sailing, and practice rigging, stowing, and so on; go canoeing, or hike to the beaver dam, or climb the nearest mountain. Take your supper along in a bag and go exploring, or blaze a new nature trail.

Compose a new camp song, plan a bulletin-board display, plan an open house for the other sections of camp, clear a new camp site, or design and make a camp flag, a signpost, or a set of collection plates for the chapel.

Plan prayers or morning worship, reclassify the library, build a "Whatizzit?" corner for the bulletin board, make decorations for a party or banquet, start a camp newspaper or write a cabin contribution for one.

Borrow the director's record collection and plan a musical evening for everyone in camp. Make up your own stories about how these compositions came to be written.

Take musical instruments to camp with you. One person with a mouth-organ or guitar can hold a camp-fire group enthralled. (They are wonderful things to have on trips too, or for spontaneous singing at the table or on a hike.)

In the more active field, there are many variations of the hike. Try a "Whatizzit?" hike (seeing how many unfamiliar objects you can identify). Name all the objects on a hike beginning with *B* (or *Y,* or *Z*). Try a flashlight hike. Or add to a hike's interest with bird watching or tree identification.

Never say to a child who asks you about things on a hike, "I don't know." Say rather, "I don't know, but let's look it up when we get back to camp." And then look it up!

Evening games are fun; even the familiar ones such as Hoist Your Sails, Hide and Seek, and Relieve-O take on a new appeal after dusk.

Have an Onion Hunt by rubbing a piece of cut onion on stones, trees, etc. Tell the contestants, "Follow your nose."

Use your imagination on old games. A slight twist to an old game and *voila!*—a new one! Best example of the universal favourite is Dodgeball; or try playing One Old Horse as a variation. The old horse consists of four or five people each hanging onto the waist of the person in front. The players in a circle around the horse try to hit the last person, who is the horse's tail. If a player succeeds, he takes the place of the front person and the tail drops back into the circle.

With all these ideas, you need never be at a loss; but remember, an idea that comes from a camper is worth a hundred from a book. Help them to work out their own. Their idea may turn out to be the same as the one you had in mind, but this way the campers thought it up!

THE CAMP-WIDE PROGRAM

The other end of the scale from the cabin program is, of course, the camp-wide program. These "big" programs occur once a week or three or four times a summer, depending upon the size of the camp. In this category are fairs, regattas, Indian days, and gypsy days. They may take the form of all-day competitions, such as Olympic day, college track meets, or marathons; or they may be evening programs only.

Most of them will be planned and run by the program director or by other experienced people, probably with the active help of the youngsters. Your job will be to engender enthusiasm, dress up if necessary, help with the leg work, and generally enter into the whole thing with such pleasure that all the youngsters follow suit.

Some ideas for "big" programs have been used time and time again without in any way losing their appeal. There are, however, new twists which can be added to enhance even those programs of the longest standing.

The *Sunday-School Picnic,* complete with the rector, curate, and Sunday-school superintendent. Dress this up by having a bull break into the field, followed by an irate farmer and the local constabulary. Some children have a real aversion to dressing up or wearing funny hats. Why not let them go to the picnic in their best camp clothes? Other young children become really frightened by a boisterous clown; let them see that it's only the friendly camp nurse dressed up. Or perhaps your group may decide that it would be a much better Sunday-school picnic if they made candy or lemonade to sell at a stall.

A *Treasure Hunt* can be given a new twist if a gypsy caravan camps nearby a few days beforehand, and on the day of the hunt the tuck (or something else of equal worth) is stolen. The "treasure" is found in the gypsy encampment, and there's your evening program!

Gold-Rush Day may be given a new twist by the manner in which supper is served that evening. Depending upon how much gold dust has been found by the eager prospectors, they may pay to eat at the Ritz with counselors acting as waiters, and soft lights and sweet music abounding; at the Sip and Bite, where they get service but no credit and very little atmosphere; or at the Greasy Spoon, where there is no service, there are no plates, and nobody cares if you eat with your fingers.

Pirates and Sailors can take on wonderful excitement if there happens to be an island handy to the camp where the pirates can hole up against attack. "Fighting" may consist of snatching a bandana from the belt or a kerchief from the head. When the battle takes place in boats, the excitement runs high.

Fairy Night, when juniors are aroused from their beds and guided (by seniors and counselors) through the moonlit woods to the fairy glen, can be a memorable experience. Have a few fireworks for this; they are most effective. Tableaux of favourite stories on the way to the glen can be impressive.

A *Flotilla* of gaily decorated boats can be as much fun as a Santa Claus parade, particularly if there is a moon, and torches are on the dock.

Smugglers' Day is a favourite in some camps. Six or eight people are chosen to be smugglers, and their job is to smuggle the Wednesday-night picnic food from the refrigerator between Wednesday breakfast and three o'clock that afternoon. They must have three meetings from the time they are selected (usually on Monday), and they must carry the minutes of these meetings on their persons at all times. Campers who suspect their friends of being smugglers must get a search warrant from the sheriff to search them. If they find no clues in thirty seconds, they must stop searching. Everyone in camp is suspect, from the director on down, and if the smugglers are not caught or the food is not found, Wednesday supper is apt to be a little lean. The smugglers who are caught are tried at the camp-fire Wednesday night.

Skits and Stunts have a real appeal when a Hollywood scout is coming to view the talent available. When he turns up in moustache, velvet smoking-jacket, and corduroy slacks, it isn't everybody who can spot the crafts counselor. Many of the less observant are thoroughly taken in, and the results are fun.

Take a country for a theme. (UNESCO or UNICEF or the various consulates have reams of material to offer.) Have floats, folk-dancing, national games and sports, and a national meal at supper; and carry through the theme during a camp-fire or social evening. Each country opens up new possibilities. Then too, your group may have ideas for improving the festivities. Perhaps you have some youngsters who have come from Europe and really know the dances of their country. Why not include these in an International Day?

CEREMONIALS AND RELIGIOUS OBSERVANCES

Camp ceremonies are found in every camp, many of them with a tradition and history of long standing. Some of these may seem strange to you at first, and you may be hard put to keep a straight face when you see your friends on the staff made up as Indians, parading around in blankets or flitting about with lighted torches. These traditions and ceremonies will not survive in any camp unless they are filled with meaning for the campers and have a real place in their memories. Therefore it is up to you to find out as much as you can about these traditions and interpret them to your campers. New ones may find it difficult at first, and their reaction is likely to be one of amusement or withdrawal. Your own attitude here is most important. Enter into these ceremonies and try to find in them the inherent values which the years have given them.

Though many camps are completely non-sectarian, there is a place in all of them for religion and religious observances of one kind or another. You have found out about these before you accepted the camp job, and are in sympathy with them. You can greatly help your youngsters to take an active part in these observances. The tendency of some adolescents to scoff at religion will receive a serious set-back when it is discovered that the counselor considers religion important. Most camps have morning prayers or worship, conducted by the director and/or counselors and campers. Plan with your campers to take the lead in one such service. Interest from you is all that is needed.

In these camp-wide programs your main job is to see that the campers in your group take an interesting and interested part. Sometimes these big events overwhelm some campers; little ones may become totally bored watching the antics of their elders in strange costumes, and be quite confused as to what it is all about. The counselor's responsibility for program is varied; but in this, as in all other aspects of camping, three things are important: the seeing eye, the understanding heart, and the willing hand.

SKITS, STUNTS, AND RAINY-DAY ACTIVITIES

CHILDREN love to pretend. They are forever acting, and with the encouragement of an understanding and imaginative counselor, dramatics can be great fun for the actors and a rich source of entertainment for the audience.

In some camps you will find a drama department with a specialist to direct this important area of program. Formal, more ambitious plays and musicals require a specialist. However, even when one is not available, there is much that you can do to encourage and retain campers' natural interest through informal dramatics. You are not seeking academy awards; you want simple plays which require a minimum of rehearsing, so that your campers can know the thrill of being part of a play.

CAMP DRAMATICS

When casting the parts be sensitive to the camper who needs the role. For some camper this may be his one chance to achieve recognition; don't let the opportunity slip by. No part should be too long or demanding. Parts that require too much memorization and preparation become labours instead of fun. Write in extra parts for everyone who wants to be in a play.

Even without the help of grown-ups, children will produce their own skits, for make-believe is a vital part of childhood. Your main function should be as an advisor, not as a director. Let the campers generate the ideas, then when they reach blocks in their planning you might suggest how their ideas can be carried out effectively. This planning phase is rich in opportunities for learning and sharing; your job is to see that they are not lost. Be sure that the skit is in good taste. Humour should not be barbed, nor should anyone be ridiculed. Humour at someone else's expense is too expensive.

Following are some ideas for informal dramatics that have worked successfully at many camps:

Camp incidents are rich sources of material for skits. The fun lies in the exaggeration of these incidents. For instance, parodies of an overnight hike, a canoe trip, a cabin clean-up, or a staff meeting can be hilarious if kept within the bounds of good taste.

Pantomime is one of the simplest yet most effective forms of drama for campers. Unburdened with lines, the young players can concentrate on acting in the grand, gesturing tradition of the silent-movie days.

Ballads that are full of action, such as "The Shooting of Dan McGrew" or "The Highwayman," are simple, effective, and require a minimum of rehearsing.

Shadow plays, another form of pantomime, are startlingly different. A wet, white sheet is hung at the front of the stage. A strong light is directed at the sheet from behind, with the actors performing between the light and the sheet. Biblical tales, the lives of historical figures, or a mock operation lend themselves to this treatment.

Dramatizations of well-known stories, fairy-tales, legends, or Biblical tales are easy to do. They offer splendid opportunities for the campers to write their own lines; or they too may be done in pantomime, since most of the audience will recognize the story readily.

Pictures that are well known—such as "The Death of Montcalm," "Nelson at Trafalgar," "Washington crossing the

Delaware," or "The Death of Caesar"—or well-known TV commercials treated either seriously or satirically, are fun to do. The audience can be further involved by having to guess what is being portrayed.

Records, the many L.P.'s now available, can be a rich source of dramatic material. The children act the parts as the narrator on the record tells the story. *Peter and the Wolf* is a fine example.

Radio Programs are interesting to do. Performed from behind a curtain or from another room, using a P.A. system, they offer the wide scope of sound effects and dramatization without the need for costumes and properties.

Improvised Dialogue can be funny or it can be a flop. Ad-libbing is full of pitfalls and must be handled with great care. However, this can be fun within a cabin group when it is done solely for the pleasure of the group itself and not before an audience.

Another way of handling this is to have the campers think of topics, write them on slips of paper, and put the slips into a hat. Each camper draws out a slip and has five minutes in which to prepare his presentation, which may be either a straight speech or acted out.

Fashion shows are fun to hold, using either past, present, or future fashions, or perhaps contrasting these in the same show.

Puppet shows can be simply or elaborately performed by the youngest campers or the oldest counselors. They require great imagination and skill and offer unlimited scope for play-writing, property work, and designing costumes and sets, plus the fun of exercising skill and creativity in making the puppets. Some campers may be expert operators, while others supply the voices. One of the oldest forms of drama, puppetry has perhaps the greatest degree of audience identification of any dramatic form.

Play-reading has been enjoying a revival professionally and is ideally suited to camp use. The actors sit on stools on a bare stage and read their parts.

Paper-bag dramatics have the advantage of lending themselves to impromptu performances. The participants are divided into groups of four to six each. Each group is given a bag into which several articles have been placed. They have ten minutes in which to plan a skit, using all the objects in their bag. Each group in turn performs for the others.

Choral reading is a dramatic activity that deserves greater attention in camps, but should be directed by an experienced leader. Group readings can be used dramatically at services, or around the camp-fire; and when two groups respond to each other across water or across a valley, the effect is impressive.

Variety or amateur nights can provide wonderful opportunities for campers to perform either individually or in groups. Recitations, musical solos, quartets, skits, stunts, juggling, tumbling, magic, or comedy are just some of the acts possible.

Pageants can either involve an evening or be extended to a whole day. Historical events lend themselves to this treatment, particularly if they can be tied in with some national or international holiday.

Fairy-tales produced by the older campers at night by fire-light for the younger campers can provide a memorable evening for both groups.

Any of these drama projects must be truly group efforts. The campers should have an active part at all levels of the production. Plan carefully on paper the costumes, props, lights, and basic movements on and off stage. Assign campers to be in charge of these matters, and help them realize how important their backstage jobs are. If you have a camper with a natural flair for directing—not bossing—perhaps he could direct the skit. A skit poorly prepared and poorly rehearsed is neither fun to perform nor fun to watch. If it is worth doing, it is worth enough time to do it well.

The cardinal principle to follow is simplicity. Create effects by suggestion. Any camp has the materials at hand from which you can improvise any property or costume required.

Sets. Crayons, tempera paints, or paper cut-outs applied to brown wrapping-paper make excellent, inexpensive sets. Ground sheets and blankets hung from a rope or wire make satisfactory curtains. In the absence of curtains, blackouts are useful ways to manage scene changes. Stagehands carrying signs can set the place or time very easily; and even signs tacked onto objects (like "tree" or "bridge") can be used without detracting from the skit.

Costumes. Ingenuity is the key to costuming. Everyday articles such as sheets, blankets, pillow-cases, aluminum foil, nighties, towels, newspapers, brown paper, cardboard boxes, ferns, paper bags, sugar bags, and potato sacks can be changed miraculously by the magic wand of imagination into robes, togas, headdresses, armour, court gowns, or turbans. A costume may be indicated rather than completed; a funny old hat worn with ordinary camp clothes, indicates a fussy lady. Fairies can appear in shorts and shirts, as long as they have wings tacked on.

Make-up. Elaborate make-up is unnecessary. If no drama department exists, you will probably be working with women's cosmetics.

For *girls* use lipstick, rouge, eye-shadow, eyebrow pencil, and powder as you would for evening wear. A small dot at the inner corner of the eye and a short red line at the outer will make the eye appear larger.

For *boys,* make the eyebrows dark and heavy and use little

rouge and lipstick. If girls impersonate men, paint on moustaches.

A look of age can be created by dusting the hair with corn starch and tracing the lines on the face with an eyebrow pencil or grease paint, as the actor smiles and frowns. Soften the lines into shadows for the most realistic effect. Humorous characters can be created by blacking out the front teeth. Raffia, unravelled rope, or wool make deceptive hair; and if it is dyed, the results are remarkable.

RAINY DAYS—OUTDOORS AND IN

While a rest is often welcome on a rainy day, being cooped up for too long only builds pressure in a cabin. Campers must have constructive outlets for their boundless energy. Rain seems to bother grown-ups far more than children. If campers are dressed properly, most activities can continue, and even take on a special zest, in the rain.

Swimming in a warm rain, canoeing, rowing, even sailing with the new Dacron sails, are all fun; and fishing is a natural for rainy days.

Hiking in the rain takes on new adventure and a different world of nature awaits you. You can go orienteering, or beachcombing for driftwood, pebbles, or fossils; you can look for tracks; and walking barefoot through puddles and squishing mud between their toes is an experience all children should have.

Rainy days afford an opportunity really to put your woodcraft skills to the test. Teach your campers how to find dry tinder and wood, build a fire, and even cook-out in the rain. Test that lean-to for leaks, or build different types of shelters and demonstrate their values and limitations. Demonstrate the importance of ditching around any shelter.

Many group games such as Hide and Seek, Red Rover,

Crows and Cranes; or mass games such as Capture the Flag, Prisoner's Base, Treasure Hunt, or Scavenger Hunt can be played in the rain.

Rain may eventually drive you indoors. Obviously, it is impossible for everyone to converge upon the craft shop and recreation hall all at once. It takes careful planning to work out a fair allocation of these indoor facilities. Meanwhile, part of any rainy day will have to be spent in your cabin or tent. Now, what do you do?

If a rainy day follows a string of hot, active days, why not sleep in and have a later breakfast? While this is a treat, it is useful too; it will help to recharge campers' batteries. Some campers may even take naps at any time during a rainy day.

These are days to curl up with a good book, reading either silently or aloud. A story-teller may unfold his tale, or someone can tell about a trip he has taken. Here is a chance to catch up on those overdue letters, or to write a story or a poem.

Solving puzzles or riddles, or playing other mental games such as Geography, Buzz, or Ghost can be fun. The group might act out a story or ballad, or make up a cabin skit or song.

Start a progressive story, stop at an exciting place, and let the next person carry on. Have you ever participated in a "whopper fest" to see who can tell the biggest lie?

There is something special about gathering around one bunk with a guitar, ukelele, or harmonica and singing together. Lying on their bunks, the rain on the roof, seems to make campers open up; it's an opportune time to discuss any topic suited to their interest.

It's fun to write out dedications or legacies for the next year's campers, wrap them in a plastic bag, and either hang them in the cabin or bury them outside, leaving only a mysterious map behind.

Every camp activity has some technical parts that can be

undertaken indoors, such as water-safety knowledge, life saving, first aid, camp craft, knot tieing, sailing rules, compass instruction, or star lore.

Bring simple craft materials back to the cabin so that campers may carry out projects—make scrap-books, fix snapshot albums, create puppets, or make a cabin sign or plaque, nature-trail markers, or some other sign needed around camp. What better time to rearrange nature collections or make star boxes?

This is a good time to get all those little chores done that have been put aside on sunny days, like sewing, darning, tidying shelves, grooming nails and hair, mending damaged gear, and other housekeeping tasks.

Now is the time to get out maps and plan your next hike or canoe trip.

Prepare a surprise party for another cabin, perhaps a big-sister tea-party for a younger group, with milk, cookies, favours, and games.

Charades, Twenty Questions, Simon Says, Earth-Fire-Water-Air, Concentration, I Spy, Hide the Penny, and Hidden Objects can provide many stimulating hours for all ages. Try blindfolding contestants and having them attempt to identify common sounds or detect objects by feel or smell. Checkers, Chess, Pick Up Sticks, Dominoes, Jacks, or games brought from home make good tournaments.

It can be a luxurious experience just lying back listening to good music on a radio or record player, or interesting hours can be spent on flower arrangements or making miniature Alpine moss gardens in glass jars.

Take advantage of these rainy days to learn parts for a play, make costumes and sets, or gather properties.

Plan now how your group might contribute to the final banquet, or think up ideas and decorations for a party to be held at a later date.

While camp-wide rainy-day programs will probably be planned by a committee or by the program director, you may be called upon to contribute ideas. Here are a few suggestions to help kindle the fires of your own imagination.

Hold a sunshine prediction pool, in which everyone writes down his guess as to when the sun will first shine again.

Prolong meal hour with a rousing sing-song, or gather around the fireplace for part-singing. Added zest can be achieved by drawing from a hat the names of different counselors to lead their special songs. A novel twist is to auction off lost and found articles for a song or stunt.

Stage a concert or talent program, or have each cabin prepare an act or skit for an amateur show. Perhaps it could be a giant TV spectacular, with silly commercials and "guests" in the audience masquerading as celebrities, or a radio program from behind stage curtains, with all the sound effects.

Hold a meal as an impromptu banquet, with hilarious "guest speakers", special favours, and "imported" entertainers. Have a camp-wide birthday party: divide the camp into groups by months or seasons according to their birthdays, divide the dining-hall into sections and decorate each appropriately, with each group preparing a skit or song.

The activity of sunny days leaves little time for theory, but rainy days provide a fine opportunity for all activity specialists to conduct their programs indoors.

Autograph Bingo is a good mixer. Everyone is given a blank bingo card and a pencil, and fills each square with the autograph of a camper, until twenty-five names have been secured. Regular bingo is then played by calling names from the camp list.

An afternoon of fun can be had by staging a carnival of games. Many games of skill can be devised by any imaginative person—for example, dropping clothes pegs into a milk bottle, bouncing table-tennis balls into an egg carton, tossing pennies into a floating saucer, pitching cards into a hat, or tossing paper balls into a waste-basket. Contestants can carry score cards or teams can compete, players pooling their scores and rotating from game to game.

Similar to carnival games is a track meet with events modified for indoor play. These, too, may be played by individuals or by teams. A few possible events are: a soda-straw javelin, a paper-plate discus, a balloon shot put, or a standing broad jump backwards. The high jump becomes blowing a feather over a bar.

A simple, active game of indoor golf can be played by tossing bean bags into large tin cans laid out like a golf course.

When energy is crying for release, have an hour of relays and active games, being careful to modify the locomotion to fit the confines of indoor play.

Other good energy tappers are the various combative games, such as leg-wrestling, cock-fighting, arm-wrestling, poison pool, two-man tug-o-war, and badger pulls.

Some old mattresses laid out on top of ground sheets make ideal mats for tumbling and pyramid building.

Folk and square dancing are ideal rainy-day activities. Girls often like grooming tips for teen-agers and health classes, including exercises done to music.

Many of the drama activities discussed above can also be used effectively as rainy-day programs.

Stimulating hours can be spent in discussions geared to different age levels, or even by conducting a formal debate, remembering to let the campers choose the topics that interest them most.

A number of long-time favourites, such as quizzes, Beat the Clock, Twenty Questions, and spelling bees always make a lively program.

A mock trial, if conducted with good taste, can make a very funny program. A courtroom setting is created with a humorous judge, an odd assortment of jurors, and lawyers for prosecution and defence. These latter two must be quick thinkers, with a gift for the humorous twist of phrase. A number of campers and staff (no one is immune) are accused of various crimes, tried, and invariably found guilty. Imaginative punishments, fitting the alleged crimes, are meted out on the spot.

If rain comes in the evening after an active day, be flexible enough to swing the program indoors for individual tent or bunk nights in which each group plans its own evening. Aim for a quiet, relaxing program, such as a pyjama party, storytelling, music listening, or quiet singing around a fire.

There is something unforgettably special about the sound of rain on a roof while you are snug inside, munching cookies and sipping hot chocolate.

Do not live in dread of rainy days at camp, for they can be wonderfully memorable. The important thing is for you to be cheerful and imaginative and have interesting ideas about what to do.

Chapter Eight

YOUR CAMPERS AND NATURE

Flora Morrison & Kirk Wipper

CAMPING means living in an outdoor world. Campers have a unique opportunity to learn to know this world, to appreciate its processes and laws and to enjoy and wonder at its beauty.

Children are fascinated by the space age; at camp they can see the planets, the stars, the galaxies. To some of these one day they may travel; but in the meantime they can feel, touch, hear and see their own planet, earth, and discover a little about its structure and the forms of life that are born, grow and die upon it.

Here children can begin the lifelong adventure of exploring the natural world. This may lead to their becoming scientists, or naturalists, or artists; it certainly can initiate an under-standing of the universe and of themselves as part of it.

City children are sometimes frightened by the outdoor world—the weird sounds of a screech owl or a loon, the sight of peculiar bugs or a darting bat, the darkness and vastness of the world, the tremendous waves and winds, the thunder and lightning of a great storm. The reassurance of an adult who can understand and explain is invaluable.

Counselors are sometimes dismayed by the thought that they must "teach nature." It used to be fashionable for young people to say, "I don't know a thing about nature," but it was untrue. Nowadays it is less fashionable, because schools have improved their courses, from kindergarten to university, in the natural sciences, and the lure of exploration is enticing young people to learn a great deal about weather, gravity, the earth's crust, and so on. Television and movies have also made nature more familiar. Of course, neither your campers nor you know everything, but you can learn; and you will be surprised to find that right now you really know quite a lot.

NATURE OUTSIDE YOUR CABIN DOOR

Suppose you and your group are sitting outside your cabin or tent. You might try these things:

First, *mark off a three-foot square* on the ground. Write down everything you observe within that area and take turns telling what you know about something you have seen. An earthworm wiggling; what questions arise? Where does he live, what does he eat, where are his children? How long is his lifetime? Is it true that he gets eaten by birds? Possibly you do not know the answers. There is perhaps a nature expert you could consult. There are certainly books in the library. Let's find out!

Next, all *look as far away* as they can, and find something between themselves and the horizon that they would like to tell about or ask about—that one little white cloud in the clear sky (where did it come from, what is it doing?); the difference between the trees at the top of a high hill and those at the bottom; the strange little objects growing out of the bare rock. What does the group know? What else can we find out?

Next, let's *watch the dusk or the dawn*. What are the first and last colours you see? Why? How do day sounds turn to those of night, and those of night to day? Put a red paper over your flashlight, and stay quietly in the darkness. What nocturnal animals come your way? Turn your red light on them; you can see them, but they won't notice the light.

(Why?) What are they doing? You may perhaps hear Mother Whippoorwill teaching her little one to whip. You may see a porcupine nosing around licking salt from a board where a human hand has sweated, or young racoons wetting their food in the lake. Perhaps there are shooting stars, or a technicolour extravaganza of the northern lights. What are these things and what causes them?

All this, and so much more, may be observed right from your own cabin, if you will stop, look, and listen. This takes time and the willingness to be quiet.

Children can grow to love animals and birds. Squirrels, chipmunks, and mice will probably be around the cabin. Possibly racoons, porcupines, rabbits, skunks, and foxes will come to visit. Beaver, otter, mink, and weasels may come by also; perhaps a deer with her fawn, or a bear. Watch them, but be sure your campers do not try to catch or trap them. Rabies has reappeared in animals in Canada and the New England states, and an untreated bite or scratch from a rabid animal may be fatal. If a camper gets bitten or scratched by any animal report it to the nurse immediately. Be particularly careful of animals who seem too tame; they may be sick. A camp is no place for caged animals; you can get to know them in their own world much better than by seeing them miserable in a man-made home.

Snakes, frogs, toads, turtles, and salamanders are interesting creatures; so are fish and clams. Watch and try to discover how they live and what they do.

Formal "bird walks," arranged for a certain time, have sometimes been boring expeditions in camps, usually because the group has been too large and the birds have flown off in holy horror. But you cannot fail to see and hear birds right around your cabin, if you are quiet. Why not wake up some morning just before dawn, and listen and look? You may hear the sounds of loons and owls, the signing-off of the whippoorwill; you may see the white-throats and warblers, a mother duck and her brood swimming by the shore, the great blue heron flying over. Possibly the camp has bird records to help you identify the sounds; certainly there will be bird books in the library.

There may be a nest near the cabin. Leave it there, and watch. When the nesting season is over, the nest may be taken down for examination. Before it is handled, it should be well sprayed with an insecticide.

Another activity you can carry on right in your cabin is to read aloud stories, or parts of books, about the outdoor world. The ones you choose will depend upon the age and interests of the group, and your own taste. Avoid those which purport to be nature books, but in which animals talk or are clothed. How they do communicate with one another and are arrayed in their own suitable covering are fascinating matters in their own right.

You might try some of Jacqueline Berrill's *Wonders of the Woodlands and Wonders of the Seashore* series, or parts of Konrad Lorenz's *King Solomon's Ring.* Sheila Burnford's *The Incredible Journey* would make a good story continued every night before bedtime. Pieces from Gavin Maxwell's *Ring of Bright Water,* the amazing tale of an otter who lived with the author, or of Franklin Russell's *Watchers at the Pond,* or Rachel Carson's *The Edge of the Sea,* or even some of the classics such as Thoreau's *Walden* or Hudson's *Green Mansions,* could be used. Also there are the nature magazines with many fascinating short articles, some slanted particularly to definite age groups.

To supplement the books in the camp library, it is a good idea to take along a few nature reference books of your own, so that they will be immediately available to your cabin group. There are good inexpensive pocket editions, as well as sturdier field guides for more permanent use. A magnifying glass and field glasses are good to have in the cabin. Of course, campers should learn to use and care for them properly.

From these experiences you will get a lot of questions from your campers—questions about sex and reproduction, death, differences among species, what birds and animals do in winter, the balance of nature, game laws, evolution. Discussions may lead you far afield. You will not know all the answers—the nature leader and the books will know more—but you will have helped develop a curiosity about nature and an interest in the creatures who are sharing their territory with invading humans.

NATURE FURTHER AWAY

Children like to explore. By foot or boat there are many places of amazing interest within a short distance from the camp.

In your meanderings, make a point of visiting different habitats: pond or stream, lake shore, open glades, lightly wooded ridge, deep, shaded forest, bog, trail, farm lands, mountains, valleys, or seashore. Help your campers realize that each of these places has living things that like their area more than any other. In time the campers will know what to expect as they pass from one sort of terrain to another. When this happens you can be sure you have done well; your campers are becoming sensitive to the natural world; they are getting in tune with the wilderness.

On such outings it is a good idea to stop, to listen, to talk and to wonder. It is also good to provide opportunities for stopping, to distribute fruit drops or biscuits or a cool drink. Or you might take along a snack, or a meal to cook. This gives you a chance to show the group where they can find good firewood. Discuss with them why some woods are better than others for certain purposes. Look at the grain and texture of the wood and note where it was found. Try to find a green tree of the same kind; look at the difference between it and the firewood. See if your campers can find other trees like it and challenge them occasionally with finding more firewood of the same kind.

On these outings you can locate some of the dangers of the outdoors. You might include poison ivy, oak, sumac, mushrooms; it is a good idea to mark samples of these to ensure identification. There are also the dangers of dry, dead trees, and of overhanging rocks on a cliff.

In time you will find your campers interested in more detail. They will want to stop and examine natural things more closely. You can help them now to explore in terms of colour, odour, touch, sound, shape, and even taste. You will find your magnifying glasses, binoculars, and even a small microscope useful. Do not push the use of these aids, however, unless there is an obvious demand for them. Leadership in the outdoors is not like teaching a science class at school.

You will also find that there will be a great urge to pick up things and take them back to camp. *Take care.* Sometimes specimens occur only rarely, and you would not want them to become extinct in your area. Unfortunately, it is often the uncommon item that provides a temptation for the camper. Better to make a project of marking the spot so that it can be visited and revisited by campers. Those who make a discovery will most certainly want to have it drawn to the attention of the others in camp.

Little has been said about knowing the names of things. You have gathered by now that this is not essential at first. The time to learn the name of a plant or animal is when it becomes inconvenient or awkward not to know it. When a camper would like to describe the specimen to someone else, the name becomes an asset.

Special Activities

Some wildlife projects can be developed quite readily. For example, there is the *wildlife trail*. In this, you and other camp people can mark a wide range of objects gradually and build up the trail over a period of time. Whenever new items are identified, you may add to the markers along your winding trail. It provides a challenge to campers if the name of a specimen is concealed or hidden by a cover.

The *terrarium or aquarium* is always popular too. It will take time and effort to make. You can find out how to do this from your camp library or the nature counselor.

It is interesting to *dissect old birds' nests* to see what they are made of.

A *bog-plant garden,* a *wild flower garden,* or a place where animal visitors can be kept uncaged for a short period are other useful ideas.

A *"what-is-it?" corner* will inevitably catch the interest of campers. Or put a new object outside your cabin, where passers-by can see it and guess what it is.

Experiments are fascinating as well. You might catch grasshoppers, gently mark them with a bright dab of nail polish, and then see if any of them can be located in one day, two days, and so forth.

The possibilities really have no limits. The important principles are to take advantage of a current interest and form it into an adventure which will capture the enthusiasm of the campers; and to do with care what you start to do, so that your materials are preserved. Keep your projects "camper size."

Games are perenially attractive. Many can be devised for improving the campers' understanding of wildlife. One excellent one, a variation of Kim's game, can be used on rainy days. Remembering a group of natural objects is one form, but blindfolded campers may also attempt to identify natural things through smell, touch, taste, or even sound. Rearranging scrambled names is another popular game. Of course, you must have in your repertoire the old favourite, nature scavenger hunt. Be careful that you do not run the risk of depleting uncommon specimens in this game. True-or-false questions, given to various teams, are designed to correct misunderstanding about wildlife. The game of "Animal, vegetable, or mineral" can be adapted to almost any age group with considerable success, as can the challenge of "Who am I?" This is another opportunity for you to make use of your imagination in inventing suitable games for campers.

Arts and crafts, emphasizing the use of natural materials, is another field to consider. Here the camper may use the item in a way that will bring out its latent beauty. It may be a root or a piece of driftwood that reminds the craftsman of a bird, animal, or plant he knows. It may be grass that can be worked into a Navaho weaving, or dry balsam that can be fashioned into a fire drill. The bark of a dead birch can become a watertight container, and the burl of a hardwood tree makes a fine drinking cup for out-tripping. Spore prints or spatter prints of fern fronds make fine artistic collections which can be mounted and kept intact for a long time. Sketching on a fungus is a creative activity which can be accomplished on a hike or camping trip and lends itself to many excellent topics, including a trip log or a pictorial record of an outstanding experience on the trail.

The adventure of *living off the land* has great appeal for experienced campers. This requires advanced knowledge of wildlife and a real appreciation of the wilderness. Remember that conservation is important, and certain edible plants should be left untouched in order to protect the future of specimens in the area. Some natural foods may be a distinct surprise to the camper. The dandelion, for example, in its early stages of growth can make a magnificent salad, rich in vitamins. Many foods the camper will learn about were used by the forerunners of modern camping: the pioneer, the *voyageur,* the fur trader, and the Indian. The experienced campers who live off the land are therefore sharing a link with a glorious historical heritage. You and your group can learn from, and be intrigued by, tales of their adventures.

Many other activities can be carried out, depending upon the camp's situation and your interests. Old farmhouses and barns will help to tell how our grandfathers lived in pioneer times; a friendly old neighbour who has "known these parts" for seventy years has tales of lumbering and fishing that may do more to arouse interest in conservation than could any expert. The rise and fall of lake level may demonstrate man's control over nature by making water reserves for electrical power systems. The lives of the people in the community— fishermen, farmers, trappers—give an introduction to the assets of the land and man's use of it. Visitors to camp who have explored in the Antarctic, or are working on space research or archaeological digs, may stimulate terrific interest in an area of natural life. This you can follow up by discussions, getting books, and becoming more interested yourself.

While even the youngest campers can be taught good conservation practices, older ones may become interested in discussing the public responsibility for preservation of recreation areas and conservation of natural resources. This links the world of nature with that of public affairs. Too, discussions of man as a part of the natural world— his evolution, physiology, and animal likeness, the development of his mind—offer many interesting hours for your older campers.

There is so much to do, to enjoy, to think about; there is so much as yet unknown of the natural world and of man's relation to it, that you and your campers should find your summer truly a "journey into wonder."

Chapter Nine

ASSISTING WITH AN OUT-TRIP

Barry G. Lowes

TRIPPING gives campers a thrilling link with our country's early days and marks the high point of the summer for most of the campers, for it is filled with adventure. It is also fraught with hazards. The group will be on its own. You must assume greater responsibility on a trip than in any other camp activity, so you will be sent to supervise or assist only if you have the necessary qualifications in the skills the trip requires. The hazards can be minimized if you plan well and follow certain basic principles. This chapter will give you some ideas that will help to make your trip safe, comfortable, and an excitingly memorable experience for you and your campers.

Tripping can influence attitudes, habits, and behaviour probably more than any other activity. It is truly co-operative living and can be successful only if each one shares the work load. Some of our veneer is stripped away on a trip and the true self is revealed. A trip is filled with teaching opportunities if you are alert to detect them.

However, not all girls are interested in tripping, and a few boys may not be interested either. Tripping should be a privilege and not a requirement, and no one should have to go. See that your cabin group does not put pressure on any camper in this respect.

There are many kinds of trips: hiking, canoeing, riding,

bicycling, or by caravan, all of which have their own pleasures. Here we will describe general principles which are important on any kind of trip, but will show how they work out in detail in canoe tripping. If your trip is of a different type, you can adapt them.

What are some of the things that you can do in the city to prepare yourself for going on trips?

Read books on woodcraft and nature. While this is no substitute for the real thing, it will help greatly.

Take a *first aid* course to learn what you should do for cuts, sprains, headaches, foreign bodies in the eyes, and such serious matters as fractures, severe bleeding, burns, apparent drowning, head injury, and clinical shock.

Think back, *remember* the most memorable experience of your own trips. How can you ensure that your campers will have some of these same experiences?

Tripping does not mean roughing it. On the contrary, the purpose is to be as comfortable as possible with as little as possible. It is you and your resourcefulness, pitted against capricious nature, full of the unexpected.

There is a trend in some camps for staff to plan, pack, paddle, double back on portages, do all the cooking, and so on. This cheats a child. Let the campers help to do everything, with your supervision where necessary. It takes longer this way, but this is how children learn; and besides, they get a thrill from doing things themselves.

PREPARING FOR THE TRIP

Planning is half the fun of any trip, so be sure that your campers have a full share in it.

It is wise for you and your campers to condition yourselves for trips by hiking, canoeing, and carrying full-weight dummy packs. You should also practise the special canoeing skills required on trips, such as how to land on rocky places, avoid snags and rocks, and paddle in rough water.

For how many days should a trip last? This depends upon the age, experience, size, physical condition, and desire of your campers. Their ambition usually exceeds their strength and ability. It is wise to add an extra day to allow for additional rest, bad weather, exploration, or any unforeseen delay.

Don't push! What's the hurry? Where are you going? If campers come back tired, hungry, dirty, badly bitten, then something is seriously wrong with the leadership.

Spread the map out on the ground or floor so that everyone can see it. Go over the route together. If it is new, have someone who knows the route go over it with the group.

Rather than just push, paddle and portage, have a purpose for the trip, such as exploring a new route, fishing, mapping the special topographical or geological features of the area, photography, preparing camp sites, searching for historical sites, or observing wildlife.

Menu planning is always exciting. Some camps will have pre-set menus to choose from. If you have complete freedom to plan your own, seek the advice of the camp dietitian to ensure nutritional balance. Write out two copies, give one to the trip-room or kitchen, and keep the second copy for the trip.

Girls are usually much more interested in cooking and making fancy meals than are boys. They will probably want to do more of the planning of menus and supplies and will look forward to spending more time trying recipes.

For girls, portaging must be carefully considered in advance. If there is a long portage a male guide is necessary, or else a man must meet the trip and handle the heavy things; this can be done by truck, but it means careful arrangements. Two *strong* girl counselors can handle a canoe for a short portage. Several trips with manageable loads are better than one trip overloaded.

Paratroopers pack their own parachutes. So, too, the person who must carry the pack over the portage should pack it. Take time to be sure that the shoulder straps and tumpline are adjusted to fit each carrier. Poorly adjusted straps cause unnecessary strain and fatigue.

There is an inevitable tendency to take too much. The following list of personal belongings, including what the camper is wearing, is quite sufficient for a four- to six-day trip: 1 pr. underwear, 1 pr. longs, 1 bathing-suit, 1 T-shirt, 1 heavy shirt, 1 sweater or sweat shirt, 1 raincoat, 3 pr. woolen socks, 1 pr. shoes, towel, toilet articles, sun hat, pyjamas.

Optional items might include: small knife, flashlight, compass, camera, fishing tackle, binoculars, notebook and pencil. *No* transistor radios!

Remember, whatever you pack you must carry. Do not have any loose articles. You need your hands free. Also, loose articles are too easy to leave behind on a portage or a camp site.

Different camps have different methods of packing, but the following seems to work in many camps. Have your campers lay out their bed-rolls or sleeping-bags with their personal belongings on top, and check the items with them. There will be no going back for anything that has been forgotten. Roll the sleeping-bag with all the belongings into a tight roll, and tie it. Two sleeping-bags go into each pack next to the carrier's back. One ground sheet lines the pack and the other covers the top before the flaps are tied down. The foodstuffs are divided equally by weight and distributed in each pack. One pack, designated the utility pack, contains the pots, tent, axe, and first-aid kits, with the first lunch right on top where it is easy to get at. For younger campers it may be necessary to use more packs, so that each will be lighter.

Your trip-room will most likely have a staples list. If you are the counselor in charge, it is your responsibility to check each item as it is issued to you and as it is packed. Do not entrust this to anyone else; then you will have no one to blame if you find that some item has been forgotten.

Each camper should have a paddle of the right length; with the butt resting on the ground, the tip of the blade should reach his mouth.

A sixteen-foot canoe will hold two packs and three people comfortably. Thus one carries the canoe while the other two carry the packs, eliminating the need for someone to double back on portages. Fasten the tumpline of each pack to a thwart. You don't plan to capsize, but if you do, you will not lose all your gear. Before setting forth test the balance of the loaded canoe. The three paddlers *always* kneel and the packs are distributed to give the best balance. If you are heading into the waves, have the bow slightly higher. If the waves are coming behind you, keep the stern slightly higher.

ON THE TRIP

Your first concern is the *safety and welfare* of your campers. See to their comfort before your own. In matters of safety your guide should be, "If in doubt, don't do it."

Three canoes make an ideal trip. Four is still workable, but more become an armada, unwieldy on portages and crowded on the camp site. Have a strong, experienced sternsman, or better still a counselor, in each canoe, and try to match canoes for paddling strength. Keep the canoes within talking distance of one another. Canoes that are strung out apart are of no use to one another, and have even been known to get lost from the rest of the trip. Set your pace by that of the slowest canoe. Draw together into a pontoon for conferences when necessary.

Be alert to changes in the weather. No one should ever be *caught* in a storm. Storms don't descend suddenly; they are heralded by certain signs. On a sunny day, beware of a hazy sky on the horizon from where the wind is blowing. Thickening cloud cover, or two layers of clouds that are travelling in different directions, can mean a storm. If you saw a ring around the moon the night before, or the stars were hazy, or the night was unusually warm, or there is a red sunrise, be on the lookout for rain during the day. Being on the lookout, you will see the storm coming. Get off the water or move close to shore. It is better to wait out a storm, or paddle farther by following the shore-line, in order to be safe. Never go on the water when there is any threat of lightning; it can be deadly.

A trip is not the place for young counselors to try to prove that they are men, at the expense of the campers' safety and health. Avoid fatigue; take frequent rests. Remember that when you feel the least bit tired, the young campers are very tired; but they will seldom admit it. Don't wait for them to ask for a rest; you must call the halts. Be ruled by consideration for the weakest. Remember that an over-tired disappointed camper will not want to repeat the experience. This may mean that he or she will be the loser for the rest of a lifetime.

Take time to look up and *see* things. Always paddle silently around points in lakes or bends in rivers and be on the lookout for wildlife. Long after the rest of the trip has receded into the backs of the campers' memories, they will still remember the deer drinking, the beaver working, or the otters frolicking. When you return to camp, ask yourself, "What did we see or do that made this trip special? What highlights will we remember in later years?"

PORTAGING

Don't run your canoes up onto the shore; come into land slowly and carefully. The bowman should get out in shallow water and steady the canoe. Unloading should be done with the canoe floating, not up on land where rocks and stubs can puncture it. A pack dropped heavily into a canoe that is resting on some submerged rock or snag can break its ribs or punch a hole in it.

Once everyone has his pack, the head tripper should lead the way, carrying a canoe. He is then able to help the campers remove their packs at the other side, or double back if necessary. Another counselor should be the last one over the portage. His job is to help the campers on with their packs, then check to be sure nothing has been left behind.

On long portages the wise counselor stops for a rest, not necessarily because he needs it, but because the campers will rest if he does. There are so many things worth stopping for on a portage: to look at Indian pipes, moccasin flowers, cardinal flowers, different types of rocks or birds, or a view through an opening in the woods; or there may be a field of wild raspberries. Let's pick enough for supper!

No one should ever get lost on a portage, but it has happened. Each person should know what to do in such an event. If the path is clear, the lost camper should retrace his steps. If he is in doubt, he should *stay put,* calling at intervals, for the group will certainly be looking for him. Wandering farther and farther astray only makes the search more difficult. (See Chapter IV.)

ON THE CAMP SITE

Find a camp site by 4:00 P.M. at the very latest. Better earlier, leaving time to pitch camp, fish, swim, explore, prepare a proper supper, and arrange comfortable sleeping areas. Rushing and pushing to beat the darkness denotes poor organization and leadership.

Campers should play the major role in conducting the trip. After all, it is their trip. They should be learning and practising constantly. Your job as counselor is to teach and help, not do it for them or lie and watch them do it alone.

When a problem arises and they ask, "What shall we do?" your reply should be, "What would *you* do?" Help them to think through problems. Don't cheat them by thinking and doing everything for them.

If everyone pitches in to make camp, there will be time for fun and relaxation. Following are some possible ways of assigning jobs that have to be done:

1. Everyone does what needs to be done. This is idealistic and seldom works in practice except with a very experienced group.

2. Assign one camper as wood gatherer, one as pot washer, etc. This system is boring and breeds the comment, "This isn't fair."

3. Assign everyone a number. As a job needs to be done, call out the next number in turn, including your own. This system spreads the work load, gives the broadest possible experience, and is fair for everyone. The campers seem to like this system.

4. Ask the campers how they would like the jobs to be allotted.

Shelter

Many types of shelter can be made from ground sheets, tarpaulins, canoes, boughs, etc., but none is a substitute for a good light-weight wall tent.

Pitching the tent on high, dry, level ground should be your first job at every camp site, even on sunny days. You will go to bed many nights looking into a star-packed sky, only to scramble for shelter during the night as the rain comes pelting down. Pitch the tent facing the breeze on warm, muggy nights and away from the wind when the weather is stormy. Do not pitch it under trees, where a dead branch might fall on it. Always dig a trench around the tent to catch the run-off water. It is work, but a must if you are going to keep dry in any rain.

Beds

Take time to arrange comfortable sleeping areas. Energy and spirits are at a high level after a good night's sleep. Don't snicker at inflatable ground sheets. The extra pound of weight to carry is little compared to the comfort afforded. Beds of balsam boughs can be soft, but on well-travelled waterways the trees would soon be stripped if everyone made one.

Test the ground where you will sleep for annoying roots, stones, ant-hills, etc. Find a level spot and shape out a depression for your shoulders and hips. Avoid beaches; they are hard and damp and can harbour stinging sand flies.

Toilet

Dig a latrine and make sure your campers use it. Locate it well away from the camp site and blaze or clear a path to it. Indiscriminate "bushing" is a practice that should never be tolerated.

Wood

Gather more wood than you will need for supper and breakfast—twice as much as you think you will need. Store the extra wood and kindling under cover ready for the breakfast fire. The best size of wood for cooking can be broken over your knee. An axe is needed only for splitting damp wood or hardwood, and one slip can be serious when you are many miles from medical aid. Keep the axe sheathed and out of sight. It should be used only by people specifically designated by the camp as being qualified.

Food

There is a saying that anything tastes good on a trip. This is not true; scorched meat is wretched wherever you eat it. The food sent out is good, and the cooking should do justice to it. Let one or two campers prepare the food under your supervision. Given enough help, they will get a thrill out of it, and this is how they learn. The amount of supervision required will depend upon their experience and ability.

Food for breakfast should be set aside and all food should be stored under cover, protected from the weather and foraging animals. Take care of your food supplies; anything lost or spoiled cannot be replaced. On each trip find time to try something special—a cake, a pie, or a new stew.

Dishes

Washing dishes is an onerous but necessary task, easier to do than to fuss about. The secret is plenty of hot water and soap. If you rub soap over the outside of the pots before using, the black will wash off easily.

Camp-fire

Anyone who has ever sat around a small camp-fire on a trip, heard the loon's call and the frogs' chorale, and seen falling stars streak across the sky, has entered the enchanted world known to few. The mood will dictate what happens— a story, a quiet song, a discussion. These are ripe moments. Don't lose them. It might be fun to read aloud tales of real explorations and canoe trips, bits from *The Lonely Land* by Olsen, or stories of life as it was in the early days in the area in which you are travelling. In well-known camping country in Ontario, girls were thrilled by reading Anna Jameson's *Winter Studies and Summer Rambles in Canada,* describing a journey in the eighteen-thirties through the lakes and streams where the girls were then travelling.

Sleep

Turn in early. A good night's sleep enables you to get an early start in the morning with everyone in good spirits.

Check your campers for warmth, comfort, and mosquito netting. Take a few minutes to talk to each one in turn. You will seldom have a more impressionable or opportune time to reach your campers.

Breaking Camp

Assign everyone a job, so that cooking, cleaning, packing, and loading can proceed simultaneously. Leave the site cleaner than you found it. Burnt cans should be flattened and buried far back in the woods or sunk well out in the lake. Be sure that you leave a supply of wood under shelter for the next group.

Be certain that your fire is out. One or two pots of water are not enough; the deep heat can travel along rootlets and break out days later. Where possible build your fire on bedrock, then float it away. When you feel satisfied that it is out, run your hand through the ashes to be sure. If you are reluctant to put your hand into them, then you had better flood it some more.

Make a final check for forgotten articles.

Some camps have the fine tradition of pausing before getting into the canoes in the morning for a moment of meditation or a "thought for the day." Don't let these valuable moments slip through your fingers on your trip.

AFTER THE TRIP

Try to return on time to avoid anxiety for those back at camp. If you will be late and it is possible to notify the camp, do so.

Bring your campers back clean. Filthy, disheveled campers are no credit to you or your camp.

Return all the equipment to its proper place. Make a group report of the trip in writing, including suggestions on how it could have been improved.

This concludes your trip. If it was well planned and conducted, the campers will have experienced a sense of fun, adventure, achievement, and comradeship, and an awareness of the outdoor world, that will live on in their memories for a lifetime. They should be eager to go out again—soon!

HEALTH AND SAFETY

Men who live in the woods—foresters, guides, and trappers—do not take chances. They know and respect the hazards of bush travel.

Teach campers that good camping is safe camping. Daring, hazardous actions known in some camps, such as travelling until late at night, shooting rapids, and paddling across treacherously rough lakes, should be scorned as poor tripping practices.

Learn and practise first aid until you feel competent to handle any emergency. Teach its skills to your campers. Better still, be safety conscious and prevent mishaps.

Be cautious of the sun; insist on hats and watch for sunburn. It can cripple a camper.

Insect bites can cause great discomfort and even sickness. Keep your campers well covered, pants tucked inside socks, sleeves rolled down, hats on, and under mosquito netting for sleeping.

Some camps draft safety rules for out-trips that are stressed constantly until they become second nature to all campers and staff.

Following are some sound examples that have proved valuable over many years of canoe tripping. Some are relevant to many kinds of tripping, and these are marked with an asterisk:

* 1. Never gamble with safety. If in doubt, don't do it.
  2. Never shoot rapids. No one ever drowned on a portage.
  3. If your canoe tips, hang on.
* 4. Stay near shore in rough weather. Stay on shore in dangerous weather.
* 5. Stay off the water when there is any threat of lightning.
* 6. No swimming except with staff supervision, first checking the area carefully for hazards, limiting the area, and using the buddy system and guards. Never dive.
* 7. No camper is to be separated from the rest of the group.
* 8. The counselors must never leave the group completely alone.
  9. Never leave any of the party on a camp site, unless you leave a canoe there too.
*10. Never play with a knife or hatchet. Use them with great care.
*11. Never play with fire or around a fire.
*12. Do not drink untreated water.
*13. Keep your food clean.
*14. Report any sign of illness immediately to the counselor in charge.
  15. Wear shoes on the camp site. Unlace shoes in a canoe.
*16. Be sure your fire is out.
*17. If you must walk along a road, stay well to one side facing the oncoming traffic, one counselor leading and one following.
*18. If a serious accident occurs, give first aid; one

counselor goes for help, one stays behind. A smudge fire built on the beach will attract a patrol plane. Notify the camp as soon as possible.

*19. Your maps should have the locations of telephones marked on them.

Remember always that you represent your camp. Wherever your trip takes you, your camp will be judged by the conduct of you and your campers, mainly on your good use of sound safety procedures.

PART III

The Camping World

Chapter Ten

EXTENDING YOUR HORIZONS

Elsie & David Palter

ORGANIZED camping in North America is just over one hundred years old. You are now part of it. You will want to know something about its growth and its main concerns at the present time; and you will also want to develop your own ideas about the direction it should take in the future.

CAMPING HISTORY

Since early days North America has been a camping country. The early explorers and pioneers lived in and on the out-of-doors. The travels of Champlain by canoe and portage opened the land which is now the heart of camping country in Eastern Canada. He even mentions the mosquitoes. The early settlements along the Atlantic seaboard were at first merely camps. The opening of the West meant adventuring into amazing new country while living under the simplest conditions. The romance and hazard of the early years of the white man's life on this continent gave birth to our love of camping; and there is nowhere better than a camp for bringing to life the adventure, enterprise and courage of those bygone times.

The first organized camp in America is said to have been started by Frederick William Gunn in Connecticut in 1861. Here two weeks of camping were included in the Gunnery

School curriculum. Between 1880 and 1890 organized camping was well under way. Ernest Balch started the pattern for private camping at Chocorua, New Hampshire, while Camp Dudley, New York, initiated organizational camping under the Y.M.C.A. In 1892 girls joined the camping movement when Camp Orey, New York, included them for a four-week period.

In Canada the Y.M.C.A. camp started in 1892 and now situated at Golden Lake, Ontario, is the earliest recorded camp in the Camp Directory. However, it is said that Fraser Marshall in the Maritimes began Y.M.C.A. camping outings in 1880. Mr. A. L. Cochrane's camp, opened in 1898 and settled in 1901 at Temagami, Ontario, was the first private boys' camp in Canada; and in 1906 Miss Fannie Case brought some American girls from Rochester, New York, to the wilds of Algonquin Park, to Northway Lodge. These camps are still in existence.

About fifty years ago, people who had been going camping decided to come together to discuss their interests and problems, and a small group of them held the first recorded camp conference in Boston in 1903. From the mutual interest initiated by this meeting, the Camp Directors' Association was founded in 1924. This name was changed to the American Camping Association in 1935. The Canadian Camping Association began one year later, with Mr. Taylor Statten as the first president.

It is rather exciting to realize that within a hundred years, from such small beginnings, camping and camping associations have grown so rapidly and widely that they now serve several million children and young people.

One of the important developments in recent years has been government support of camping. Camping areas have been set aside and supervised, training courses organized, plans for suitable camp buildings published, and camps constructed by public funds and rented to various organizations at a reasonable cost. Governments and camps have begun to work together on preservation of historical and beauty sites and on conservation of natural resources.

From its beginning, camping has focussed its efforts on helping children experience the values of living in and enjoying the out-of-doors, and making use of the fascinating and bountiful natural resources and vast spaces of this continent. Camps started originally as individual enterprises and only gradually began to work in association with one another. Within this association, camps have retained to a high degree their individual flavour. Your camp may be quite different from the one your friend attends. It might be wise if you asked your camp director about the origin and development of your own camp and what he considers its particular purposes to be, and also about other types of camps. Perhaps you could arrange to visit and discuss some of these.

The camping associations now include camps sponsored by private individuals, and by organizations, churches, and institutions. They may be all-boy or all-girl camps; or two camps under the same management, one for boys and one for girls—the brother-and-sister type; or they may be co-educational, taking both boys and girls. They vary also in the range of age of campers they take. Some camps specialize; the major emphasis may be on music, drama, foreign languages, riding, canoeing, campcraft, or sailing. Day camps have sprung up in the past twenty years, in or near cities or towns. Some children participate in a day-camp program for part of the summer, and then attend a resident camp for the remainder of the time.

The desire for travel has found expression in mobile travel camps, operating in different locations; the campers are on the move by rail, truck, air, horse, or cycle. Such travel camps are not limited to this continent; some American camp directors have organized trips to foreign countries. Family camping is undergoing a change, and more comfortable and appealing facilities are being made available in government-operated camp sites. There are also specialized camps today for such groups as physically handicapped and emotionally disturbed children.

Some sites are being used throughout the year for school camping and winter camping. Adult camps, including those for older citizens, often operate beyond the summer months. Week-end camping for disturbed and delinquent children has proved to be valuable for adult understanding of these children, and for the children's understanding of themselves.

Throughout the years many new activities have been added to the program. Instruction in water skiing was a rarity about twenty-five years ago, but is commonplace today. More recently, the lists of camp equipment and activities include trampolines, scuba diving, and electronics. Some people wonder whether the variety of activities which has been added to the camp program does not destroy its original purpose—the enjoyment of simple living in the out-of-doors. They also question the desirability of elaborate buildings and de luxe equipment. These are matters which you will enjoy discussing with your camp director, and you will certainly hear them debated when you attend meetings of your local association. Your opinion is important, of course, because it is your generation that is going to decide the trends of the future.

CURRENT CONCERNS OF CAMPING

A number of important matters are being discussed in camping today. You should think about these and acquire as much knowledge about them as possible, so that you may express an enlightened opinion.

The first is the matter of *standards*. For a quarter of a

century camping people have been trying to develop standards without imposing standardization. Dr. Hedley Dimock, under grants from the W. K. Kellogg Foundation, called a group of leading camp people together in the early nineteen-forties to discuss, and come to some agreement on, what they considered to be "minimum standards and desirable practices for camps." Their recommendations were issued in a booklet and studied intensively in many of the local associations.

Legislation requires that standards be met in certain areas of camping. Camps must conform to the general laws of the land, of course, and they must meet the regulations specifically directed to camping. These now pertain mainly to health, sanitation, safety, liability, employment, insurance, and taxes.

Above these the American Camping Association has established further standards regarding programs and personnel. Before a camp can become an accredited member, it must be visited and have its practices approved as complying with the standards of the Camping Association. The "Report of Camping Practices" used by the American Camping Association deals with eight aspects of camping: Personnel, Program, Camp Site, Facilities and Equipment, Administration, Safety and Transportation, Health, Sanitation.

Not all the Canadian provincial camping associations have as yet accepted compulsory visitation, but some that have not done so have adopted a voluntary program of visitations. This is intended to enrich and strengthen the operation of camps, and to enlighten the public, and parents in particular, about the importance and meaning of camp standards.

Some camping people feel that the most important aspect of camping is that of personnel or *leadership*. Qualifications for camp directors, supervisors, instructors, and senior and junior counselors are constantly being debated. What minimum age, education, and experience levels should be required? Should every camp leader have special camp training? Good directors know that without good leadership it matters relatively little how elaborate the buildings are or what modern sanitation is installed. There is no greater responsibility than that of looking after other people's children. Wise, educated and trustworthy people are needed for the job.

Your opinions regarding standards will be important to the future of camping. So you might well begin thinking and discussing what the good values are, and how standards may be established without standardizing camps—that is, making them all the same.

CAMPING, EDUCATION, AND SOCIAL ORGANIZATION

At camp everything seems to be so informal and full of fun that it may be hard for you to realize that professional people in such fields as education and psychological and sociological research regard camping with great interest and seriousness.

Children learn very quickly at camp; they learn how to paddle and to swim, to take part in a play, to take responsibility for their own possessions, and to co-operate with others. This is because they are interested in what they are doing and enjoy their various experiences, even those which require hard work and difficult effort. Interest has proved a most effective spur to learning at camp, and educationalists often consider how to adapt these successful methods to general education. One leading Canadian educational psychologist said, "If the patterns of a good camp could become the basis for public education, we could do a miraculous job in one generation." You might well consider how some of the effective methods of camping could become part of the teaching system of schools and universities.

Then, too, camp is a society; here the campers and staff live together with relatively little intrusion from the outside world. Here the problem of social relationships is the same as in society at large, but on a smaller scale. Camp provides an ideal opportunity for achieving a society which increases the well-being of every individual and develops a plan of co-operation.

Of course, camps differ in their approaches to the matter of social planning. In some, even now, the director makes all decisions and controls all activities. There is little opportunity for any other individual to express or practise his own ideas. Other camps profess that campers are permitted to do exactly as they like at all times. However, most camps attempt to develop a social organization in which democracy is used as a way of life. Each person from the youngest camper to the director is allowed freedom to develop and express his ideas, and is encouraged to use these for the welfare of the group as a whole. Children are not merely *taught* principles of democracy; they *live* democratically within limits of health, safety, and the general camp philosophy. They have a real share in the running of the camp.

Wilbur C. Hallenbeck of Teachers' College, Columbia University, has said, "One of the things most devastating to human personality is that characteristic of our modern world which has deprived individuals of their right to have something to say about what happens to them." One of the objectives of the American Camping Association is: "To give emphasis in camping to citizenship training in keeping with the principles and traditions of American democracy." Camps may yet help to point the way to a constructive method by which the good society will be created.

You might discuss policy of camp government and consider how some of the ways that work in camp could be effectively used in the wider community.

IN SUMMARY

In one hundred years camping has grown from a few

summer outings in the woods to an important influence in the fields of education and social enterprise. This growth has depended basically upon the vision of camp directors and their ability to secure capable and enthusiastic camp leaders. The future growth of camping depends upon these very same things, for no movement can be greater than the quality of its leaders. Being a camp counselor requires constant insight and imagination, for you must have sufficient vision to understand that upon the guidance you give your campers today depends the citizenship of the world tomorrow.

The challenge which the first directors and counselors answered so well is now up to you. What future trends will be, what children will be served, what standards will prevail, what part camping will play in education and research and what influence it will provide in world affairs will depend upon your decisions, your concern, and your values. As camping people we are dealing with the most precious of commodities—human personality. The acknowledgement of the dignity and worth of the individual is the core of our civilization, and we in camping have the opportunity and privilege of contributing towards the future.

Bibliography

GENERAL

Brown, M. W., *It Takes Time to Grow*. Toronto, United Church Publishing House, 1953.

Colby, C. G., *First Camping Trip*. New York, Coward McCann Inc., 1955.

Dimock, H. S., and Hendry, C. E., *Camping and Character*. New York, Association Press, 1929.

Duran, C. A., *Program Encyclopedia*. New York, Association Press, 1955.

Fletcher, Margaret I., *The Adult & The Nursery School Child*, University of Toronto Press, 1959.

Gibbon, J. Murray, *The Romance of the Canadian Canoe*. Toronto, Ryerson Press, 1951.

Graham, Abbie, *Working at Play*. New York, The Woman's Press, 1941.

Hamilton, Mary G., *The Call of Algonquin*. Toronto, Ryerson Press, 1958.

Hammett, Catherine T., *Your Own Book of Campcraft*. New York, Pocket Books Inc., 1952.

———and Musselman, V., *Camp Program Book*. New York, Association Press, 1950.

Harbin, E. O., *The Fun Encyclopedia*. Nashville, Abingdon Press, 1940.

Hartley, R., and Goldenson, R., *The Complete Book of Children's Play*. New York, Thomas Y. Crowell Co., 1957.

Jenkins, G., Schacter, H., and Bauer, W., *These Are Your Children*. Chicago, Scott, Foresman & Co., 1952.

Jersild, A. T., *Child Psychology*. Englewood Cliffs, Prentice-Hall Inc., 1960.

Kepler, H., *The Child and His Play*. New York, Funk and Wagnalls Co., 1952.

Mitchell, A. Viola, and Crawford, Ida B., *Camp Counseling*. Philadelphia, W. B. Saunders Co., 1950.

Northway, M. L., and Weld, L., *Sociometric Testing: A Guide for Teachers*. University of Toronto Press, 1957.

Perry, Ronald H., *The Canoe and You*. Toronto, J. M. Dent & Sons (Canada) Ltd., 1948.

————*Canoe Trip Camping*. Toronto, J. M. Dent & Sons (Canada) Ltd., 1953.

Prendergast, W., *Recreation Time*. Toronto, J. M. Dent & Sons (Canada) Ltd., 1950.

Thurston, LaRue A., *Complete Book of Campfire Programs*. New York, Association Press, 1958.

Webb, Kenneth, *Summer Magic*. New York, Association Press 1953.

————*Light from a Thousand Campfires*. New York, Association Press, 1960.

REFERENCE BOOKS

Burt, W. H., *A Field Guide to the Mammals*. Boston, Houghton Mifflin Co., 1952.

Eifert, V., and Metcalfe, B., *Native Ferns*. Toronto, Canadian Audubon Society, 1953.

Golden Nature Guides: Birds, Trees, Stars, Flowers, Insects, Mammals, Seashores, Reptiles and Amphibians, Weather, Fishes, Rocks and Minerals. New York, Golden Press.

Hillcourt, W., *A Field Book of Nature Activities and Conservation*. New York, G. P. Putnam's Sons, 1961.

Klots, A. B., *A Field Guide to the Butterflies*. Boston, Houghton Mifflin Co., 1951.

Lutz, Frank, *A Field Book of Insects*. New York, G. P. Putnam's Sons, 1935.

Morgan, A. H., *A Field Book of Ponds and Streams*. New York, G. P. Putnam's Sons, 1930.

Murie, Olaus J., *A Field Guide to Animal Tracks*. Boston, Houghton Mifflin Co., 1954.

Peterson, R. T., *A Field Guide to the Birds*. Boston, Houghton Mifflin Co., 1947.

Pough, F. L., *A Field Guide to the Rocks and Minerals*. Boston, Houghton Mifflin Co., 1953.

Storer, J. H., *The Web of Life*. New York, New American Library and Mentor Books (paper eds.).

Thomas, W. S., *A Field Book of Common Mushrooms* (rev. ed.) New York, G. P. Putnam's Sons, 1948.

Wherry, E. T., *Wild Flower Guide*. New York, Doubleday & Co. Inc., 1948.

Zim, H. S., and Baker, R. H., *Stars*. New York, Golden Press, 1956 (paper ed.).

NATURE

Burnford, Sheila, *Incredible Journey*. Toronto, Little Brown & Co. (Canada) Ltd., 1961.

Berrill, Jacquelyn, *Wonders of the Seashore*. New York, Dodd, Mead & Co., 1951.

———*Wonders of the Woodland Animals*. New York, Dodd, Mead & Co., 1953.

———*Strange Nurseries*. New York, Dodd, Mead & Co., 1954.

———*Wonders of the Wild*. New York, Dodd, Mead & Co., 1955.

Logier, E. B. S., *Snakes of Ontario*. University of Toronto Press, 1958.

———*Frogs, Toads, and Salamanders of Eastern Canada*. Toronto, Clarke, Irwin & Co. Ltd., 1952.

Maxwell, Gavin, *Ring of Bright Water*. London, Longmans, Green & Co., 1960.

Miller, Richard B., *A Cool Curving World*. Toronto, Longmans Canada Ltd., 1962.

Milne, Lorus J. and Margery J., *The World of Night*. New York, Harper & Bros., 1956; New York, Viking Press (paper ed.).

Olson, Sigurd F., *The Singing Wilderness*. New York, Alfred A. Knopf, 1956.

————*The Lonely Land*. New York, Alfred A. Knopf, 1961.

Russell, Franklin, *Watchers at the Pond*. New York, Alfred A. Knopf, 1961.

Thoreau, H. D., *Walden Pond*. New York, Doubleday & Co. Inc. (paper ed.).

MAGAZINES

Camping Magazine: Official journal of the American Camping Association, 181 Chestnut Ave., Metuchen, N.J.

Canadian Camping: Official magazine of the Canadian Camping Association, 170 Bloor St. West, Toronto 5, Ontario.

Canadian Nature: Canadian Audubon Society, 423 Sherbourne St., Toronto, Ontario.

The *Bulletin* of the Federation of Naturalists, Edwards Gardens, Don Mills, Ontario.